"It takes half a lifetime to realize what all spiritual masters have taught us—that true power comes from the synthesis of opposites. Save yourself a lot of time and read this remarkable book!" —John Bradshaw, author of *Bradshaw on the Family* and *Homecoming*

"A lovely, amazingly clear book." —Eugene Gendlin, author of *Focusing* and *Experiential Psychotherapy*

"Its quiet voice, wise, compelling, speaking to both clients and therapists, is remarkably effective." —David Loye, author of *The Sphinx and the Rainbow*

"An illuminating book that balances, corrects, and complements the healing wisdom of analytic and problem-solving Western psychotherapies." —Howard Clinebell, author of *Basic Types of Pastoral Care and Counseling* and *Well Being*

"A joy...like breathing clear mountain air. As I read it from the viewpoint of either therapist or client, I felt safe—in a world I could trust, sure that I would be understood and have the space to grow." —Albert Pesso, author of *Movement in Psychotherapy* and *Experience in Action*

"*Grace Unfolding* is an inspirational book for every person in ministry and psychotherapy to read as a reminder of our true calling." —Jeanne D. Weikert, *Journal of Pastoral Care*

"*Grace Unfolding* has reinspired me to listen more closely, to allow myself as both therapist and client to move only in accordance with the *what is* that is taking place." —Lynn Vaughn, *Transactional Analysis Journal*

GRACE UNFOLDING

Psychotherapy
in the Spirit of the
Tao-te ching

GREG JOHANSON
AND RON KURTZ

with brush paintings and
calligraphy by
CHARLES CHU

Bell Tower
New York

Grateful acknowledgment is made to the following for permission to reprint:
Macmillan Publishing Company for excerpts from The Way of Lao Tzu *(Tao-te ching)*
translated by *Wing-tsit Chan. Copyright © 1963 by Bobbs-Merrill.* HarperCollins Publishers *for excerpts from* Tao: A New Way of Thinking *by Chang Chung-Yuan. Copyright © 1975 by Chang Chung-Yuan and from* Tao Te Ching *by Lao Tzu, translated by
Stephen Mitchell. Copyright © 1988 by Stephen Mitchell. Alfred A. Knopf, Inc., for
excerpts from* Lao Tzu/Tao Te Ching *by Gia-fu Feng and Jane English. Copyright ©
1972 by Gia-fu Feng and Jane English. Ballantine Books, a division of Random House,
Inc., for excerpts from* Lao-Tzu/Te-Tao Ching *translated by Robert G. Henricks. Copy-
right © 1989 by Robert G. Henricks. Penguin Books Ltd. for an excerpt from* Tao Te
Ching: The Book of Meaning and Life *by Lao Tzu, translation by Richard Wilhelm,
translated into English by H. G. Oswald (Arkana, 1985), English translation copyright ©
Routledge & Kegan Paul, 1985. Shambhala Publications, Inc., 300 Massachusetts Ave.,
Boston, MA 02115, for excerpts from* Tao Teh Ching *by Lao Tzu, translated by John C.
H. Wu. Copyright © 1961 by St. John's University Press, New York.*

Published by Bell Tower, an imprint of Harmony Books, a division of Crown
Publishers, Inc., 201 East 50th Street, New York, New York 10022. Member of the
Crown Publishing Group.

Random House, Inc. New York, Toronto, London, Sydney, Auckland

Bell Tower and colophon are trademarks of Crown Publishers, Inc.

Originally published in hardcover by Bell Tower in 1991

Manufactured in the United States of America

Design by Suzanne Noli

Library of Congress Cataloging-in-Publication Data

Johanson, Gregory J.
    Grace unfolding : psychotherapy in the spirit of the Tao-te ching /
Greg Johanson and Ron Kurtz ; with illustrations and calligraphy by
Charles Chu. — 1st ed.
        p.   cm
        1. Psychotherapy. 2. Lao-tzu. Tao te ching.   I. Kurtz, Ron. II.
Chu, Charles. III. Title.
RC480.5.J58   1991
616.89'14   dc20   91-6584
                                                                       CIP
ISBN 0-517-88130-6   10 9 8 7 6 5 4 3 2 1   First Paperback Edition

This book is dedicated to
Edgar N. Jackson, Jung Young Lee, and Nelson S. T. Thayer,
for their inspiration in pioneering new paradigms
while respecting the wisdom of the old;
and to Leif and Lily,
for their wisdom in helping adults know
when it is time to play.

Special thanks to literary agent Bob Silverstein
for his encouragement and vision
in bringing this volume into being;
to Platt Arnold, Nancy Donny, and Hope Johanson
for the generous gift of their editing skills;
and to Toinette Lippe, our Bell Tower editor,
for bringing such passion, precision, and good judgment
to this as well as all her projects.

The highest good is like water.
Water gives life to the ten thousand things and does not strive.
It flows in places men reject and so is like the Tao.

Thirty spokes share the wheel's hub;
It is the center hole that makes it useful.
Shape clay into a vessel;
It is the space within that makes it useful.
Cut doors and windows for a room;
It is the holes which make it useful.
Therefore benefit comes from what is there;
Usefulness from what is not there.

—Tao-te ching; *from chapters 8 and 11,*
translated by Gia-fu Feng & Jane English

CONTENTS

INTRODUCTION

The Great Way is very smooth and straight;
And yet the people prefer devious paths.
(Wu, 53)

Some say that my teaching is nonsense.
Others call it lofty but impractical.
But to those who have looked inside them-
selves, this nonsense makes perfect sense.
(Mitchell, 67)

Sometime during the sixth to fourth centuries B.C. the mysterious Lao Tzu bequeathed
us the *Tao-te ching,* a book which would
become the foundational text of the spir-
itual/philosophical school of Chinese
thought called Taoism. The identity of Lao
Tzu ("old master") is lost in the mists of
time. Tradition says he was a senior contem-
porary of Confucius, a government archivist
perhaps, who reluctantly put together this
book of wisdom for the benefit of those who
governed. Although more than one hun-

dred English translations of Lao Tzu's work have been made, it has generally retained its Chinese title, *Tao-te ching*. In English this might be rendered as "The Classic *(ching)* of the Way *(Tao)* and Its Virtue *(te)*." The *Tao-te ching* is a mystical or spiritual book because it presents the Tao, or the Way, as the source, truth, or creative principle behind all the appearances of life. Like God in the Western tradition, the Tao can never be captured in words. A practical, philosophical training manual, the *Tao-te ching* encourages us to embody virtue, to live lives that are consistent with the reality of the Tao. With poetic grace it seeks to help us bring our being and our doing into harmonious unity.

Lao Tzu's teachings were written during a time when old structures were declining. Trade and business were growing with the advent of new technologies. Rulers flaunted their power, developed new weapons systems, and called for law and order to quiet the restless masses. Confucianism, the philosophy of the day, emphasized the values of conformity and worldly treasure. Life was both busy and unhappy.

Into this volatile and complex situation that seemingly called for much to be done, Lao Tzu introduced the ideas of nonbeing, nondoing, and nonviolence. Nonbeing was a revolutionary concept for the Chinese. It has also been a difficult concept for Westerners because it does not mean "nothing" or "emptiness" as the Greeks and those that followed them understood it. For Lao Tzu, nonbeing is the foundation of being, more like "everything" than it is like "nothing." Like the hub of a wheel or the hollow of a cup, it is the empty space that makes things useful. Nonbeing gives being the space to exist. An analogous thought is found in an ancient Jewish myth that says in the beginning God was everything, so the only way God could create was by withdrawing, disappearing, to allow the space for life to emerge. Nonbeing suggests not identifying with a part of anything, or of ourselves, but embracing all, excluding nothing. Similarly, nondoing for Lao Tzu does not mean doing nothing, but rather not interfering, doing only those things which are natural and in line with the movement of our ever-changing world.

Nonbeing and nondoing were such radical notions that no one knew what to make of them. In a possibly apocryphal story, Confucius is said to have had an audience with Lao Tzu. Afterward he commented, "Lao Tzu is like the dragon, which is beyond my knowledge." Still, the unmistakable rightness of Lao Tzu's teaching was intuitively recognized. It became a powerful though subtle underground influence, continuing through the centuries until the present. Lao Tzu pointed to the simple and unforced, to a gentle influence rather than effort or struggle. For him, nondoing was not a way to withdraw from involvement with life, but rather a way to achieve realization in life through actively and consciously maintaining harmony with the Way Things Are.

Together, nonbeing and nondoing support nonviolence. Nonviolence is an attitude of trust in the creation, especially the natural changes which flow from the interaction of being and nonbeing. It is a commitment to not interfere with the processes of life, but to celebrate their spontaneous, organic intelligence. Nonviolence promotes a respect for the subtle, almost imperceptible movements of mind, body, and spirit, and gives rise to a yielding or softness which follows and nourishes these movements rather than correcting or conquering them.

The spirit of nonviolence manifests itself in a particular way of knowing that Buddhists, after Lao Tzu's time, named mindfulness. Mindfulness is a state of alert but relaxed consciousness. It does not restrain, add to, or interfere with what comes into awareness. It is a form of bare attention that is receptive and that enhances our awareness of whatever is. Mindfulness is a powerful therapeutic tool for studying how we create our perceptions of the world. It is a courageous and honest encounter with current reality, with what simply *is* at the moment.

Lao Tzu was both a severe critic of the institutions of his day and one who offered positive alternatives. Our intent here is to reflect on how the spirit and principles flowing from his *Tao-te ching* can illuminate and guide the practice of psychotherapy in our day and time, one similar to his. We make no attempt to be comprehensive. Rather, our aim is to allow a few notes from his wisdom to reverberate in heart and mind. A number of disguised case examples are provided. They are meant to evoke the flavor, style, and technique of practicing psychotherapy in a way that is congruent with the principles of the *Tao-te ching,* and to emphasize how Lao Tzu's wisdom can provide a foundation and framework for inventing whatever technique is useful in a particular moment.

We write for both clients and therapists in the belief that there need be no secrets. The more we know about therapy as clients, the better chance we have of joining our therapists in an alliance for healing growth. The more we know as therapists, the better equipped we are to help clients receive the most from their therapeutic opportunities. The more we all know about the Tao, the more we can embrace the essential paradox that makes therapy possible: On the one hand we realize that something must change. The nature of life *is* change. We need simply to be aware of the changes and move creatively with them. However, if we were never to change, it would be all right. Our worth as people is not on the line. We are all children of the Tao, even if we are living in destructive, hurtful ways. While our spirits yearn for the greater freedom, integration, and connectedness that psychotherapy can help us discover, we tend to resist growth in any context that suggests we will be acceptable only when we have achieved that freedom and connectedness. The grace of a therapeutic setting is meant to protect and affirm our spirits in their essential goodness. This affirmation may then set us free to envision and create life-fulfilling changes, and to acknowledge and explore our barriers to more satisfying living when they arise.

Although we write for clients, therapists, and other interested readers, our primary perspective is that of the client. As such, this book is a personal letter from us, the authors, to current or would-be clients. It expresses what we have found helpful in our own experiences as clients. We hope it enables others to find satisfaction in therapy. We encourage clients to refer back continually to their own wisdom in terms of checking the truth of their experience with ours.

The form of the book is both continuous and discontinuous. In commenting on selected texts from the *Tao-te ching,* we have followed the traditional order of the chapters, while including quotes from later chapters when they fit in with the themes discussed. This does not lend itself to the kind of linear discussion we are used to in the West, since there is a circularity to Asian writing suggestive of the interconnectedness of all thought.

Many fine translations of the *Tao-te ching* exist. We quote from a few of our favorites. What chapter a text is from and which translation is being used are indicated in parentheses.[1] Lao Tzu valued the feminine principle in a special way. Stephen Mitchell acknowledges this in his translation by having the master or sage alternate between being male and female. Other translations have an all-male sage. Since the majority of *Tao-te ching* quotations we include are masculine, we have given many of the therapist examples a feminine voice. To achieve inclusive language we often use the plural to avoid writing "he or she" and "his or her," though admittedly that is not the happiest solution for those who love the Queen's English.

Individual chapters of the book can be read by themselves, although there is a thread of continuity woven from the beginning to the end that builds on itself. We suggest approaching *Grace Unfolding* in a meditative way. Read a

---

[1]Translations are from Wing-tsit Chan *The Way of Lao Tzu*; Chang Chung-yuan, *Tao: A New Way of Thinking*; Gia-fu Feng and Jane English, *Tao Te Ching/Lao Tsu*; Robert G. Henricks, *Lao-Tzu Te-Tao Ching*; Stephen Mitchell, *Tao Te Ching*; Richard Wilhelm, *Tao Te Ching: The Book of Meaning and Life*; and John C. H. Wu, *Tao Teh Ching*. Interpretive paraphrases by Ron Kurtz are also used.

chapter slowly. Be open to allowing it to strike chords of agreement or disagreement with your own experience. Be curious. Explore whatever enters your awareness. Take the time to embrace the echoes and associations that emerge. A thought, feeling, sensation, or memory that arises may lead to something else you will find useful in your process of self-exploration. Trust that the Tao is working through your reading experience, stirring the waters within you.

Finally, we realize that as authors we are in trouble right from the start, for as the *Tao-te ching* puts it,

Those who know do not talk.
Those who talk do not know.
(Feng & English, 56)

Greg Johanson and Ron Kurtz
The Hakomi Institute, 1991
Boulder, Colorado

NAMING

有名

The Tao that can be told is not the
eternal Tao;
The name that can be named is not the
eternal name.
The Nameless is the origin of Heaven
and Earth;
The Named is the mother of all things.
(Chan, 1)

From the outset the *Tao-te ching* points to both the inevitability and the inadequacy of words. In psychotherapy the words we use both give rise to and kill meaning. Words can name and create meaning, bringing experience to expression and understanding. However, they never capture precisely what *is*. We can get lost in words. They can separate us from experience, imposing alien meanings on it instead of being congruent with it. Experience is basic, even though without words we cannot articulate it.

To be the best clients we can be, we need to look within and pay close attention to our experience. We need to hesitate to name our experience too quickly, thereby imposing meaning on it and losing a chance to learn from it. It is best when we can focus on our level of being and be ready to stay there without words until the experience itself gives rise to the words.

An example: Linda went to a therapist feeling low. She said that she was sad. The therapist invited her to turn her awareness inward toward her sense of sadness, study how it registered in her body, and notice if her bodily experience said yes to the word "sad" as a precise description of her state. Maybe "sad" was the appropriate word. If so, there would be what Eugene Gendlin, the creator of the Focusing Method, calls a "felt sense" of rightness. A shift in our experience takes place when we find the right word to describe it. When we are called by our correct name, or our experience is correctly named, we relax and breathe easier from being understood. For Linda, however, "sad" was not quite the right word. Her body said that it was close, but a little off. As she stayed with her experience, allowing it to tell her more about itself (as opposed to her telling it, or her therapist, what it was), the word "grieving" arose. "Yes," her experience said, " 'Grieving' is the word that fits." Linda had a self-authenticating experience of discovering an aspect of her truth. This live connection enabled her to go even further into who she was, who and what she was grieving for, and what she needed. If she had labeled her experience too quickly with the theory of sadness, she would have separated herself from her inner reality and might never have come to know or understand the grief that was a part of her. The Tao is life, connectedness, not abstraction.

AFFIRMING THE DARKNESS

> *Yet mystery and manifestations*
> *arise from the same source.*
> *This source is called darkness.*
> *(Mitchell, 1)*

Mystery is the source of understanding. By definition, we cannot learn from what we already know. That is why so much psychotherapy is boring. It deals in the stories, justifications, rationalizations, ideas, and theories that we already know. Reading the same newspaper for the ninetieth time is neither interesting nor useful.

Though its simplicity seems insignificant, none
in the world can master it [the Tao]. . . .
As soon as there are names, know that it is
time to stop.
(Chan, 32)

When something is mysterious, it doesn't quite have a name. For instance, we may experience a slight *sense* of uneasiness in our chest. If we can resist analyzing this to purge it of its uncontrollable namelessness, it may lead us to fuller understanding. Simply befriending the uneasiness—not trying to change it in any way, allowing it to emerge more fully—leads, perhaps, to our experience saying yes to the words "fear of conflict." These words are not imposed by our minds. They arise from the mysterious region of not-knowing. Since we are attending receptively to the movements of our consciousness, other information naturally gathers around our uneasy fear. The additional meaning may emerge that we are in danger of selling ourselves short again. We realize we have been contemplating accommodating to the wants of another who we think cannot tolerate the expression of our independent desires. At this point we can choose to explore further our fear of expressing ourselves with others. We can enter deeper into its mystery and *allow it to lead us* to what is causing the fear and, ultimately, to what that fear requires to assure itself that self-expression can be both possible and useful.

Darkness within darkness.
The gateway to all understanding.
(Mitchell, 1)

ENTERING THE MYSTERY

Ever desireless, one can see the mystery.
Ever desiring, one sees the manifestations.
(Feng & English, 1)

To enter into the mystery where learning can occur, both desire and control must be relinquished. The desire to be right must give way to openness and receptivity to that which is.

Not needing to make things happen, one
understands deeply.
Needing to make things happen, one learns
about practical matters.
Core and surface are parts of the same whole.
It is in being open and innocent that the
possibility of understanding arises.
(Kurtz, 1)

An impulse to eat when we are not hungry does not need to be conquered or controlled. If we simply become curious about it and pay it friendly attention, it can become a vehicle for self-exploration. Justin had such an impulse. As we consider this example and ones that follow, remember that we are not in a linear discussion leading deeper into the process of therapy. It is more like a simple therapeutic process, which we are examining through different facets of the *Tao-te ching*. As it is illuminated from a number of perspectives, we gain a greater sense of its unity, and its integration with the larger Tao of life.

Justin was encouraged to explore his eating impulse. He experimented by slowly reaching out as though to take food, and then deliberately holding his arms back. As he did this he paid attention to everything that happened—what feelings, sensations, words, thoughts, memories, and impulses spontaneously arose. By doing this he entered into the mystery of his experience and simply followed wherever it led. He was not controlling, producing, or forcing something to happen. He was just being a witness, as though standing by a pond and watching the ripples caused by a fish breaking the surface.

The jumping fish is the thought of reaching. The pond is Justin's conscious awareness. The ripples are whatever happens in relation to the thought experiment. The witness is that part of Justin and us that can stand back and notice what is going on internally, without being unconsciously caught up in it. Mechanically reaching for food and eating is qualitatively different from observing, studying, and exploring the impulse to reach. The ability to reflect on our actions is something we as human beings can do that machines cannot.

As Justin undertook this conscious, reflective exploring in relation to his reaching impulse, a sense of urgency emerged into his consciousness. The urgency became a new mystery for him. He explored the quality of this urgency through noticing things like how it registered in his body and what feelings attended it, and the awareness dawned that he felt the need to eat to shore up his sense of strength. Strength for what? he wondered. For meeting the expectations of the next situation, his consciousness responded. Then he began to understand what had been driving him. He habitually and automatically mobilized himself around a need to meet the expectations of others. Realizing that made him feel sad. When Justin investigated this sadness he discovered that part of himself which believed that he was not acceptable to others unless he went along with what they wanted. This belief had been organizing his experience to produce the impulse to eat and the other things he had become aware of. When he simply paid attention to the experience, without trying to change it or control it through analyzing or categorizing, he was able to learn from it. He discovered that what was taking place both on the surface and deep within were connected.

WELCOMING

> . . . *the Master acts without doing anything*
> *and teaches without saying anything.*
> *Things arise and she lets them come;*
> *things disappear and she lets them go.*
>
> *(Mitchell, 2)*

The sage or master works without judgment. She is a welcoming presence who can allow for and embrace all being and nonbeing. Her response to us if we said, "I can't think now" would probably not be, "Yes, you can think. Come on now. Think!" but, "Listen to that part of you that can't think.  Perhaps it will tell you more about itself." The sage simply attends to and accommodates what is, especially those things which arise spontaneously in our experience. This attitude of acceptance, inclusion, and trust in what is, is not a technique so much as a wordless principle. The sage is not adding anything to the process, but just encouraging communion with it. The attitude is an expression of nondoing. The sage claims no credit for having created something when we begin to understand what is behind our block to thinking. We are simply empowered by what is, and can move on in a way that does not depend on the therapist's cleverness or insight.

> *She has but doesn't possess,*
> *acts but doesn't expect.*
> *When her work is done, she forgets it.*
> *That is why it lasts forever.*
> (Mitchell, 2)

EMPTYING

Therefore, in the government of the Sage:
He empties their minds,
And fills their bellies.
Weakens their ambition,
And strengthens their bones.

He constantly causes the people to be with-
out knowledge and without desires.
If he can bring it about that those with
knowledge simply do not dare to act,
Then there is nothing that will not be
in order.

(Henricks, 3)

Lao Tzu suggests that people gain greater satisfaction and strength when the sage can help them empty their minds of ambitions, desires, and assumptions. For many of us therapy must begin through an emptying process. Meister Eckhardt said that we do not find God through a process of addition but by a process of subtraction.

Learning consists in daily accumulating;
The practice of Tao consists in daily diminishing.
(Wu, 48)

When we are in therapy we need to tell the therapist a little bit about our story so that we feel that there is a bridge of understanding built from which exploration can proceed. It is also a way of communicating what we already know and hope for. However, it is not helpful to pour out theories, explanations, illustrations, justifications, and stories on top of stories. This tends to engage our minds alone, which are often already overloaded, defended, and ruled by habitual responses. Analyzing and talking *about* our lives, as if giving a report about past events, does not encourage contact with our core. Our core is that central, usually unconscious place within us that controls how we experience events by filtering what comes to us through previously constructed beliefs about life.

Experience is closer to our core than analysis—concrete, passionate, immediate, felt experience. Our core is most readily reached by emptying our minds of theories and turning our awareness inward toward present experience. Therapy can move from dialogue with a therapist about our life in the distant or immediate past to an exploration of our present, inner lives through cultivating what Buddhists call mindfulness.

Becoming mindful has to do with letting go of ambitions to control, solve problems, or achieve something. Instead we choose to bear witness. A witness, as suggested in the analogy of watching ripples in the water, is passive in the sense of deliberately not manufacturing anything. Rather, a witness is willing to observe, be receptive to, and learn from whatever arises. Willful desire to confirm and support what we already know gives way to a willingness to suspend judgments and agendas. We enter into the confusion and mystery of whatever is happening with a curious, experimental attitude, not knowing what might be discovered, but welcoming, appreciating, and savoring whatever it is. We slow down, and let go of automatic reactions that normally tell us what something is and what it means. We often lose track of time and space, like a child caught up in the wonder of playing. Like play, mindfulness explores and discovers. Though this witnessing results in an alert and aware state of consciousness, it is vastly different from ordinary consciousness in which our awareness is oriented outward; narrowly focused and intent on accomplishing some goal; fast, automatic, and habitual; and structured by a context of time and space.

A good therapist invites us, as well as herself, to practice mindful nondoing. If we report, "I'm anxious," questions like "*Why* do you think you're anxious?" produce only analysis filled with effort. There are many ways to encourage a receptive, mindful, nondoing consciousness. These ways are all variations on questions or instructions that direct us back to our experience as the only possible source of knowledge: "What is the quality of the anxiety?" "Where do you experience the anxiety in your body?" "What movement does the anxiety want to promote in you?" "What does this anxiety tell you about what you need in order to feel less anxious?"

If, as clients, we can practice staying with our experience, observing it without losing touch with it, and reporting on it without coming out of it, the experience has an opportunity to deepen. Then one experience will lead to another and the process will move from surface experiences to core beliefs which generate and organize these experiences. This movement has a live quality to it of entering new territory. Neither client nor therapist is bored. Through the joint discovery of long-buried memories and the events and lessons that formed our basic beliefs, compassion and respect are generated. It is usually easier for us to witness our inner experience with our eyes closed. Most people do this quite naturally, shutting out the distractions of the external world for the moment, allowing themselves to focus awareness more clearly on their internal world.

> *When they think that they know the answers,*
> *people are difficult to guide.*
> *When they know that they don't know,*
> *people find their own way.*
> *(Mitchell, 65)*

EMBRACING EXPERIENCE

和光同塵

> *The Tao is empty (like a bowl).*
> *It may be used but its capacity is never*
> *exhausted.*
> *It is bottomless, perhaps the ancestor of*
> *all things. . . .*
> *It becomes one with the dusty world.*
> *(Chan, 4)*

Lao Tzu treasures the value of emptiness and nonbeing. It is a positive concept. Nonbeing has great utility.

> *Thirty spokes converge upon a single hub;*
> *It is on the hole in the center that the use*
> *of the cart hinges.*
>
> *We make a vessel from a lump of clay;*
> *It is the empty space within the vessel*
> *that makes it useful.*
> *(Wu, 11)*

There is no devaluing of the empirical world here. The world comes out of the Tao. In chapter 42, Lao Tzu says:

Tao produced the One.
The One produced the two.
The two produced the three.
And the three produced the ten thousand things.
The ten thousand things carry the yin and embrace the yang,
and through the blending of the material force they achieve
harmony.
(Chan)

The Tao is the source of all life, its ever-changing complexity, and the unity which generates a natural progression from the simple to the complex. Atoms join to form molecules. Molecules join to form complex organisms. Human beings join to make families, which join to make higher and higher levels of community. Though the world can sometimes appear as less than appealing (as dust), Wing-tsit Chan comments that "Taoism in its true sense calls for identification with, not escape from, such a world" (Chan, p. 105).

Therapy, therefore, has a cosmic basis for encouraging us to open ourselves to the experiential reality of what is, and in the process, to let go of our assumptions of what must be that may separate us from it. When we enter into a witnessing state of consciousness, we do not end up talking about experience from a distance. Nor do we get caught up in the drama of experience. Rather, we become fully present to our experiential reality, while at the same time our inner witness stands back and curiously studies its nature.

In nondoing therapy the therapist follows and shepherds our state of consciousness so that mindfulness is fostered. More and more we become able to mine the wisdom of our inner experience. The therapist intervenes minimally, attempting to help by not being too helpful. As long as we are in contact with our experience, allowing it to lead us where we need to go, the therapeutic process is happening and our awareness of life is increasing. The therapist becomes everything to us by becoming nothing, by simply being present with us as we savor and are nourished and informed by life itself, by the Tao. When we are having difficulty allowing ourselves contact with what is, the therapist can help reestablish safety or provide experiments in awareness—gentle interventions that enable us to reconnect with the thread of experience that was leading us into deeper levels of awareness. Awareness and experience, the bottomless bowl through which the Tao feeds us.

REGARDING

仁

Heaven and Earth are not humane.
They regard all things as straw dogs.
The sage is not humane.
(Chan, 5)

Can Lao Tzu really mean that the sage is not
humane? Yes. The sage is not trying to be
humane, good, beautiful, wise, or anything
else. She is just trying to be who she is.
Similarly, conducting nonviolent, mindful
therapy has nothing to do with being a nice
person. Considerations of "nice" and "not
so nice" invite comparisons, dependence,
and a false sense of worth for both therapist
and client. Heaven and earth do not make
such distinctions. The rain falls on the just
and the unjust. The sage-therapist is simply
doing things organically, moving with
whatever wants to happen at deep levels,
joining with the process of the universe in
creating greater wholes out of fragmented
parts.

Our relationship with a therapist can sometimes be confusing. Chögyam Trungpa, the Tibetan Buddhist teacher, said that "the basic work of health professionals in general and psychotherapists in particular is to become full human beings and to inspire full human-beingness in people who feel starved about their lives." His lesson for us as prospective clients is to find a therapist who we feel somewhat approaches a full human being, and who also inspires us. This quality does not have a particular look or set of rules. It just feels a certain way—full of being alive and willing to share that with us.

Such therapists are inevitably compassionate and attractive. They may have no particular qualms about revealing themselves to us and appear friendly. They may be more reserved and withdraw to allow us sufficient space and silence to come forward ourselves, not wishing to get in our way. In either case, they may seem to be the kind of caring, intelligent, free people that it would be nice to go sailing with or join for breakfast at a cafe. They would be good to have as friends. We might even desire them as lovers. Why not?

Although they may relate to us in a natural, friendly way, their calling is not to be our friends or lovers. Their job, for which we pay them, and for which they feel accountable, is to encourage full and free human-beingness within us. That task is something of which they are always mindful while they are relating to us. It makes it inappropriate for them to do things that center on their own needs, although they would not be practicing therapy if they did not receive satisfaction from it. To become our lover would inescapably involve the therapist's own needs. This would also compromise the absolute safety we need to feel that therapy sessions are dedicated to our process and growth alone. We cannot close our eyes and focus attention on our inner life when we have one eye focused outward, literally or figuratively, on the therapist's needs in relation to ourselves. In addition, there are numerous possibilities for psychological damage if therapists take advantage of their position of power to gratify their own needs. Any sexual advances by therapists should be clearly seen and dealt with as inappropriate.

Someone once became upset with Trungpa at a retreat and said to him, "I'm very angry with you." With his characteristic twinkle Trungpa replied, "That's like being angry at the mirror for being fat." On one level this must have been painful and frustrating. His response did not sound friendly. On another level, the reply was the most healing one possible. Trungpa was inviting the person to self-reflection which could help him in his ongoing pilgrimage. Like Trungpa, therapists are not friendly for the sake of being friendly or being liked. Although genuine feelings of love, care, respect, and appreciation for us naturally arise as they accompany us on our pilgrimage, they are not looking or asking for mutuality. They don't take everything we say and do personally. They are centered on their task.

Therapists are present in different ways at different times for different people. However, they are constantly making careful judgments about what is happening or can happen to encourage our growth in human-beingness. This is their main criterion for acting: Will what they do or not do in the moment be helpful in our study and discovery of ourselves? Will it support our healing and growth?

Over time, as we build greater trust and depth in the therapeutic relationship, it becomes highly intimate. As clients, we often project onto the therapist a way of being that comes more from our personal construction of the world than it does from what is objectively happening. As we begin to see how we have organized the world in painful, distorted ways, and as we explore new possibilities for reorganizing in more realistic, nourishing ways, we may unconsciously test out the new possibilities on our therapist. Can this person really be here for me, so I don't have to do it all myself? Can this relationship really survive if I bring my anger to it? While we are simply free to be who we are, as conscious or unconscious as that may be, it is the therapist's job to be as conscious as possible and to use elements of our relationship with her for the sake of our growth in human-beingness. It is her job to invite us to reflect on the way we are relating to her at certain junctures, and not simply let us assume that we are grounded and experiencing things as they are. In ordinary conversations and relationships, the invitation to this kind of reflection is not part of the usual contract, and so it may appear unfriendly or callous at times.

CREATING

The Tao is called the Great Mother:
empty yet inexhaustible,
it gives birth to infinite worlds.

It is always present within you.
You can use it any way you want.
(Mitchell, 6)

Lao Tzu teaches that the Tao is always present within us in an infallible way that we can
make conscious use of. We are creative beings. We can participate in the Tao in such a
way that we become aware of the changes of
life and envision new possibilities for ourselves and the world. The *I Ching (Book of
Changes),* the foundational metaphysical
book of the East, explains more about the
nature of change. It says the Tao gives rise to
 yin and yang. Yin and yang represent the
feminine and masculine, passive and active,
contracting and expanding dimensions of
life through whose interaction movement or

change comes about. Where yin and yang meet they always produce a third. The continuous arising of the opposite of one thing to balance another, which balance generates a new third reality, is the basis for the constancy of change in life. The Tao

> is called the subtle and profound female.
> (Chan, 6)

This is not because of passive, withdrawn qualities. Female, for Lao Tzu, has to do with production, reproduction, transformation, with continuous, evolving, wonder-full creation. This female dimension that is available to us is the basis of our creative abilities.

Since we possess such creative capacities, humor can and should be an integral part of therapy. If we were not creative, if we were a broken machine that needed fixing, then it would not be compassionate to laugh with us in response to our predicament. However, as many schools of psychology, such as the Object Relations school, also affirm, we *are* creative. There is a level at which we organize both our experience and expression before they consciously happen. It is a considerable accomplishment to form an entire life drama around being withdrawn, self-protective, or conscientious. The laughing Buddha is a wonderful and compassionate image in response to such artistry. Our own laughing says we recognize that we are the creators, not the victims.

Being creative doesn't mean our pain hurts any less. Sometimes pain is an appropriate part of life. We are hit by a rock and it hurts. Our child dies and we grieve. In relation to therapeutic issues where we are manufacturing our own pain, the pain must be understood as a failure of creativity. The response to a certain situation has rigidified. We have lost our ability to create new responses for new situations. We do not understand how we have participated in creating our pain. We are no longer able to recognize new situations when they occur. Perhaps we generalize the experience of nonnourishing people in our early life and come to the conclusion that all people are nonnourishing, that nobody is willing to be there for us. When people appear to be nourishing, we find ways to doubt it, and may even be frightened by it. We end up starving in the midst of a banquet.

The *I Ching* counsels certain responses in relation to paradigmatic life situations. As one situation inevitably evolves into another, a new response is called for. When we fail to move with the new situation, there is a failure of creativity. The compassion of the therapist, sometimes expressed through laughter, can affirm the presence of our buried resourcefulness, whereas a response of pity would be an affirmation that we do not have what it takes, that we need a white knight to save us. Pity participates in the illusion which arises when the generative and inexhaustible aspects of the ever-present Tao are ignored.

An American trainer was conducting a ten-day workshop in Europe with a co-leader who was translating for him. The workshop began after lunch. One way to begin a workshop is with a round of introductions. There were some twenty-five people in the group. About halfway around the circle a woman who was a therapist and group leader herself began to tell the group that she had worked in a mental institution where she had had many clients. One day, while she was eating lunch, one of her clients killed herself by jumping from the roof. She fell right past the therapist as she was eating. As she told this story, she was becoming more and more emotional, breathing fast, crying a little, almost on the border of sobbing. Her behavior didn't seem completely genuine to the trainer. It felt more as if she was purposefully working herself up for some reason. Maybe she thought that was what the workshop was all about—getting emotional and "catharting." As she finished, she was poised, it seemed, for a huge emotional release, for entering directly into the *Sturm und Drang* of alienated life and passions. When she had completed her story she looked at the translator co-leader. Everyone else in the room looked at him too. There was a pregnant silence. Then the translator looked at the

American trainer. The whole room shifted its gaze toward him. After a long pause, he shrugged his shoulders and said, "Okay. New rule. No jumping from the roof during lunch." The co-leader made the translation and, after a moment of confusion, the woman and the whole room burst out laughing. That was the end of the drama. It sent a message that the workshop would not be pushing for emoting, that there would be plenty of spontaneous feeling to work with, and that life would be enjoyed as it continually changed and flowed from the tragic, to the mundane, to the hilarious.

COMMUNING

*The reason why Heaven and Earth can
endure and last a long time—
Is that they do not live for themselves.
Therefore they can long endure.*

*Therefore the Sage:
Puts himself in the background yet finds
himself in the foreground;
Puts self-concern out of his mind, yet finds
that his self-concern is preserved.*

(Henricks, 7)

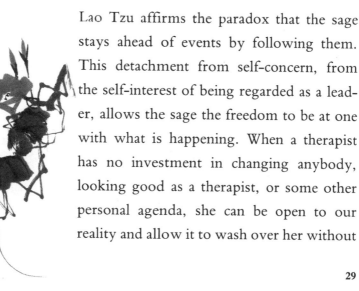

Lao Tzu affirms the paradox that the sage
stays ahead of events by following them.
This detachment from self-concern, from
the self-interest of being regarded as a leader, allows the sage the freedom to be at one
with what is happening. When a therapist
has no investment in changing anybody,
looking good as a therapist, or some other
personal agenda, she can be open to our
reality and allow it to wash over her without

prejudice or defense. As Gestalt therapist Fritz Perls once expressed it, she can be the bull's-eye the arrow hits every time. With this freedom she can follow closely the expression of our experience and use this sensitivity to guide us precisely where we want to go.

> The sage has no fixed [personal] ideas.
> He regards the people's ideas as his own.
> (Chan, 49)

Because goals, judgments, and attachments have been abandoned, her oneness with what *is* yields enjoyment and fulfillment. A form of being-in-the-world emerges which goes beyond issues of character formation to communion with the creation.

For instance, Nancy made a contract with a therapist to explore the anxiousness she experienced both when meeting new people and dealing closely with old friends and family. When she came to the initial consultation, the therapist asked her what it was like for her to be there. Nancy reported that she noticed a little nervousness, but that it was okay. She felt she could override it and get on with what she assumed the agenda was of working on meeting new people. The therapist did not forge ahead. She had no fixed plan, nor did she have any desire to prove her ability to work with relational problems. She had a sense of connection with Nancy's nervousness which was in the forefront of Nancy's awareness. The therapist chose to fall in behind it by inviting Nancy not to override it, but to befriend it by listening to it more closely.

Nothing clear about the nervousness emerged for Nancy. The therapist asked if she could identify how it was registering in her body. Nancy became aware of its location in her chest, near her heart. As she stayed with this experience, she became aware of a combined sense of anger and embarrassment. As she slowed down and allowed the contours of this sense to emerge more fully, the meaning of it clarified. It had something to do with being angry at not wanting to be hurt by others, and at the same time, feeling a sense of shame or embarrassment that she was making judgments about them. It transpired that she needed to know that she could make matter-of-fact judgments about how trustworthy people were to deal with certain revelations about herself. Furthermore, she needed to affirm that this did not mean she was calling into question other people's worth as human beings.

The therapist had a sense of being in communion with Nancy throughout the process. Both ended the session with a sense of fulfillment that comes from just being at one with life as it is, and realizing that the things life requires are usually very simple and basic. Therapists who enjoy their work in this way, and trust the Tao to provide, do not burn themselves out attempting to control things for their own and/or their client's benefit.

> *Is it not because [the Sage] has no self-interest,*
> *That he is therefore able to realize his self-interest?*
> *(Henricks, 7)*

MAKING PEACE

The highest form of goodness is like water.
Water knows how to benefit all things
without striving with them.
It stays in places loathed by all men.
Therefore, it comes near the Tao.
(Wu, 8)

Lao Tzu favored images of water, space, emptiness, femaleness, and the uncarved block. These images evoke the ideal of simplicity, lack of ego involvement, and being clean, but it is important for therapists not to get caught up in these images in such a way that another ego-centered ideal of themselves is promoted. It is easy to substitute puritanical tyrannies about not doing this or that for other tyrannies such as being pure, in the know, or enlightened. A tyranny is still a tyranny.

For therapists, part of being themselves is being aware of and befriending their own limitations, their own "mere humanity," with its ambiguities, fallibilities, and desires for success and esteem. It means knowing their own dispositions to withdraw from others, long for others, or confront and overpower others, and knowing their own fantasies of remaking the world in an image closer to their liking. When they witness these tendencies, making peace with how they have both helped and hindered them, they identify with a part of themselves that transcends character (the part of us that organizes our experience and expression in life habitually through normally unconscious belief patterns). They have no need, therefore, to justify themselves or to pretend to be someone they are not. This lack of pretense creates an atmosphere of safety and arouses our respect and appreciation.

As Trungpa suggests, it is important to find a therapist who has dealt with his own fallibilities and grandiosity since this forms a vital part of what we ourselves need to do as clients. When we sense that a therapist is not at peace with himself, that he is somehow justifying, defending, or promoting himself (unlike water which benefits us without argument, and makes no attempt to hold the higher ground), it is a danger signal. We should pay attention to these intuitions of danger or unease. It is true that a therapist who is bound up in his own character strategies can sometimes be helpful to us and that no therapist is completely unbound. A great deal of good therapeutic work is done by imperfect people, which is all of us. Some good outcomes happen by mistake, for reasons completely outside the awareness of the therapist. Often there is underlying goodwill that overcomes a lack of judgment or insight. However, if we sense that a therapist is working with us inappropriately and cannot back off because he is too self-involved, we need to feel free to act.

Perhaps sharing directly with him what we are sensing can help the situation. The therapist may take our observations and allow them to correct the process. Perhaps he will stick to his course and suggest we are resisting or that we will realize the wisdom of his way later. That makes it tricky. Certainly we are capable of misperceiving and resisting when we are afraid. Certainly the therapist's job is to make professional judgments, as opposed to accommodating our every wish and whim. On the other hand, the therapeutic process will not go anywhere productive if we do not feel safe, if we do not trust the process. Good therapists, who deliberately or naturally work within the nonviolent spirit of Lao Tzu, generally do not allow power struggles between themselves and their clients to continue once they become obvious. If there is some kind of fearful resistance on our part, they will incorporate it into the therapeutic process itself. If there is simply disagreement between what we want and what they feel they can offer, they will set us free to seek what we want elsewhere: with no blame, no guilt, no subtle messages that we need to stay to take care of them and their need to be good therapists.

If a therapist persists in using the power of his position to keep us going in a direction we don't feel is helpful for us, we may need to break off the relationship. Learning to trust our own inner wisdom is where therapy is leading us anyway. However, terminating the therapeutic relationship without the benefit of some mutual debriefing and closure with the therapist could leave us with unfinished business. If we do not believe we can have a satisfactory ending interview with the therapist by ourself, we may want to invite along some family member, friend, or advocate who can help interpret. No worthwhile therapist will have a problem with that. If he does, we may have to leave without saying goodbye and debrief the broken relationship with others. In the short run we do not need to debate whether we are right or wrong. We can be content knowing that leaving was necessary given the situation. In the long run, what is important to deal with will emerge and we will have other opportunities to attend to it. In the end, we want a relationship

with a therapist in which we can both affirm with Lao
Tzu that,

> *When you are content to be simply yourself*
> *and don't compare or compete,*
> *everybody will respect you.*
> (Mitchell, 8)

EMPOWERING

Withdraw as soon as your work is done.
Such is Heaven's Way.
(Chan, 9)

The work of therapists is not analogous to that of engineers or artists. Therapists do not create something they can stand back from, look at, and claim as their own. Mindful, nonviolent therapy simply helps us discover and affirm the wisdom of our inner experience. When insights emerge, attachments are released, new roads are discovered, and bodies reshape around more realistic, nourishing beliefs, it is not the therapists' doing. It is not their baby. Therapists' work is more like that of a midwife. They coach nature. When the baby is born, there is no question to whom it belongs.

[The Tao] accomplishes its task, but does not claim credit for it.
(Chan, 34)

In chapter 17, Lao Tzu says that when the sage is at work, people will say "we did it ourselves" (Chan). This is empowerment. Who is it who looks inside herself, explores the mystery, suspends old reactions, experiences the pain, and explores integrating new ways of being into her everyday world? Who else but the client. The therapist is blessed by being a witness, by carrying the water, by celebrating the new birth. It is enough. The task is done. It is time to withdraw. Anything else will sow confusion and induce a sticky, harmful dependence.

> *If you want to accord with the Tao,*
> *just do your job, then let go.*
> *(Mitchell, 24)*

SUPPORTING DEFENSES

抱一

Can you concentrate your vital force
and achieve the highest degree of
weakness like an infant?
(Chan, 10)

Can you love people and lead them
without imposing your will?
Can you deal with the most vital matters
by letting events take their course?
(Mitchell, 10)

The suppleness of a young child's body is contrasted here with the rigidity of an adult's. The image of water comes to mind again, water that accommodates a rock in the stream, but is not frustrated in its destination, the image of aikido as opposed to karate.

Nothing in the world
is as soft and yielding as water.

Yet for dissolving the hard and inflexible,
nothing can surpass it.
(Mitchell, 78)

One of the most vital, hard, and inflexible matters to arise in the psychotherapeutic process is resistance. Is this a place therapists can love and lead without imposing their will? Our natural western impulse is *to do* something to move people beyond the place where they are stuck. This often takes the form of some kind of confrontation, interpreted to us as clients as "for our own good."

The confrontation may take the form of encouragement. "Come on now. I know it's scary, but you can face it. You don't need to cover your eyes. You can look at this issue further." Confronting the muscular tightening that accompanies whatever fears our mind is remembering or concocting is also possible. "Your shoulders are curved in, immobilizing your arms. Here, let me press my thumbs into the knots that are doing that (or put you in a position that stresses the muscular configuration) to break through this tightness and see what is underneath it." Confrontation can occur over the correctness of an interpretation of this resistance. "I hear you when you say you are not aware of holding back anger, but angry is the way you are coming across." Most crude and disheartening is outright judgment and blame. "Until it becomes important enough for you to explore this issue, we won't be able to progress." Sometimes therapists simply give up, hoping that the issue will come around again when the client is more willing and able to deal with it.

The *Tao-te ching* does not recommend confrontation.

> *Whoever relies on the Tao in governing men*
> *doesn't try to force issues*
> *or defeat enemies by force of arms.*
> *For every force there is a counterforce.*
> *Violence, even well intentioned,*
> *always rebounds upon oneself.*
> *(Mitchell, 30)*

In Taoism this is the principle of mutual arising. Confrontation automatically brings into being a counterresistance. Although this may provide emotional drama, therapy does not progress by setting up a fight between therapist and client. As clients, we will never be able to keep our awareness inward on our experience if we need to guard against confrontation. Safety will be lost and trust in inner, organic wisdom forsaken.

The *Tao-te ching* is never simply negative. Here, it provides clues for an alternative course.

To yield is to be preserved whole.
To be bent is to become straight.
(Chan, 22)

Do the Non-Ado.
Strive for the effortless.
(Wu, 63)

Thus he [the sage] supports all things in their natural state but
does not take any action.
(Chan, 64)

I dare not advance an inch, but rather retreat a foot.
This is called marching without moving,
Rolling up one's sleeves without baring one's arms,
Capturing the enemy without confronting him.
(Wu, 69)

Less and less do you need to force things,
until finally you arrive at non-action.
(Mitchell, 48)

The movement of the Tao consists in Returning.
The use of the Tao consists in softness.
(Wu, 40)

The suggestion here, whose worth is born out in clinical practice, is that resistance be supported in the state in which it naturally arises. Paradoxically, the process can go forward through retreating and actually supporting defenses. If we cover our eyes, therapists can help us cover them, adding their hands to ours, saying verbally or through their actions, "You don't have to see anything you don't want to see." If our shoulders are turned in, imprisoning an impulse to reach out or strike out, therapists can physically take over holding in the shoulders for us. They thereby safeguard and support the prison, even provide it, which in turn can allow us to identify with the prisoner, the part of us that is saying, "Hey! I want out of here!" If we hear a voice in our head saying, "I can't do what I want without hurting their feelings," the therapist can say this for us, allowing us to be aware of whatever else is present.

One therapist in a group took over the voice that arose in Sam's head. The voice said, "Better not let people get too close!" The therapist asked Sam to teach him how to say it so that it sounded the way Sam heard it inside. He then repeated the words, with the correct inflections, while inviting Sam to be mindful and simply witness whatever reactions occurred. Sam noticed a vague anger. Studying the quality of his anger led Sam to a suspicion that people might use his feelings and vulnerabilities to manipulate him. A memory arose of his parents using his fear to get him to do something he did not want to do. A wounded child was evoked that had made a strategic decision many years before: he had better get other people before they get him. Sam discovered he needed the assurance that people would not use his feelings against him before he could let them get close to him.

If you want to shrink something,
you must first allow it to expand.
If you want to get rid of something,
you must first allow it to flourish.
If you want to take something,
you must first allow it to be given.
This is called the subtle perception
of the way things are.
(Mitchell, 36)

This subtle process of taking over voices, tensions, gestures, or postures participates in nondoing by supporting whatever is arising without adding anything new. Therapists take over doing only those things we are already doing for ourselves. They thereby increase our sensitivity level to our internal signals by lowering the physical and psychological background noise. This happens because the safeguarding of the defense, while not stirring up a confrontation, ensures a sense of safety in which we can relax.

The female always overcomes the male by tranquility.
(Chan, 61)

In the end, by going slowly, respectfully honoring the organic wisdom behind the arising of the defense, and not requiring anything particular to change or happen, the process often resolves quickly and easily. We see the situation we need to see. The woman with immobilized arms contacts the part of herself that is buried and wants to break out. The person hearing the injunction not to act without the approval of others discovers the part of him that knows his own life should belong to him.

> *Tao invariably takes no action, and yet there is nothing left undone.*
> *(Chan, 37)*

For the therapist, all this is a matter not of passively withdrawing, but of consciously not performing any unnatural actions, of moving in accordance with what is taking place.

> *If kings and barons can keep it [the Tao], all things will transform spontaneously.*
> *(Chan, 37)*

> *Tao never makes any ado,*
> *And yet it does everything.*
> *If a ruler can cling to it,*
> *All things will grow of themselves.*
> *(Wu, 37)*

When the therapist acts out of this faith and trust, not as a matter of technique, but out of truly principled living, we unconsciously recognize it. Cooperation with our unconscious is established. The process unfolds effortlessly in the direction of growth and healing. In therapy, effortful work is a warning sign of disharmony with what is organic. Both clients and therapists can recognize the sense of effort, of pushing or going against the grain, that is distinguishable from the normal work that happens.

> *How does the sea become the king of all streams?*
> *Because it lies lower than they! . . .*
>
> *Therefore, the Sage reigns over the people by humbling himself in speech;*
> *And leads the people by putting himself behind.*
>
> *Thus it is that when a Sage stands above the people, they do not feel the heaviness of his weight.*
> *(Wu, 66)*
>
> *She goes ahead of the people,*
> *and no one feels manipulated.*
> *The whole world is grateful to her.*
> *(Mitchell, 66)*

OPENING

Precious things lead one astray.

Therefore the sage is guided by what he
feels and not by what he sees.
He lets go of that and chooses this.
(Feng & English, 12)

The sage in Lao Tzu is exquisitely aware of colors, tones, textures, smells, flavors, and the meaning of words expressed, but knows that they can be misleading. So, she retains and trusts an inner source of knowing in addition to information from the senses. When the therapist invites us to be open, receptive, and mindful, she herself does this also. Her voice becomes softer, slower, curious. She allows our being and experience to become her meditation. While she observes, it is with a soft focus. Our reality washes over her. She watches the waves of sensation, emotion, and memory that run through her as she experiences us. She does not filter out anything negative or unpleasant, but values it all as important information.

Open yourself to the Tao,
then trust your natural responses;
and everything will fall into place.
(Mitchell, 23)

As she gets to know us in this reflective way, she can begin to share our experience. She may invite us to become aware of something that was not quite in our consciousness. Cheri's therapist wondered aloud if Cheri was aware of a tension in her stomach. When Cheri turned her awareness inside to see what was there, she discovered the tension, wondered about it, and watched it for a little while. The therapist then observed that the image of a black hole kept arising in her. She asked if it might be connected with anything Cheri was experiencing. Cheri said she did not have the sense of a black hole so much as a watery, swirling vortex. The therapist suggested that she study the quality of this vortex while continuing to watch the tension in the stomach. Eventually Cheri discovered that she felt that even in the womb she had been participating in her mother's worry about how hard life would be for them both once she was born, and that she herself was chronically tense at the thought of leaving the safety of a home, a job, or a relationship to move out into new areas. She also discovered what she needed to do to allow herself more freedom in this predicament.

To reach this point it was important for the therapist to trust her own inner vision and to offer her intuitions, although the signs she picked up might have been imperceptible to anyone else present or watching a videotape of the session. It was equally important that she relinquished her specific image when Cheri connected with her own inner vision, and that she trusted the validity of Cheri's experience by following where it led.

If the sage would guide the people, he must serve with humility.
If he would lead them, he must follow behind.
(Feng & English, 66)

EMBODYING

The reason why I have great trouble is that
I have a body. . . .
He who values the world as his body
may be entrusted with the empire.
He who loves the world as his body may
be entrusted with the empire.

(Chan, 13)

All things flow from the Tao. There is no dualism in Taoism that would cut off the body as evil. As in Christianity, however, the body (flesh) is sometimes a metaphor for ego-centeredness, for an attitude of separation from the whole.

Because of the interrelatedness of all things, the physical body can be seen as a reflection of the mind. Therapy can be body-centered in the sense of using the body as a royal road to the unconscious, in the same way that dream or relational material can be used. Working the other way, the body can also affect mental-emotional well-being. Attention needs to be given to imbalances in the body's structure and metabolism, its needs for movement and exercise, and its exposure to environmental toxins.

Therapy addresses splits in consciousness: splits within the mind, and splits between the mind and body. As Ken Wilber, the transpersonal psychology theorist, points out, there is also a split to be healed between the whole mind-body-self and the surrounding world.

Ralph came to a workshop in how to read bodies for psychological information. During the workshop he stood up so that the trainer and class could read his body and think of ways to help him use it as a vehicle to understand his psychospiritual beliefs. Ralph had one very interesting feature: He stood with a raised chin, as though he were looking down his nose at the world or saying, "I don't care; I'm above all this."

The trainer was not interpreting people's bodies for them, but finding ways to guide them into an experience of themselves. So he invited Ralph to turn his awareness inward and notice what happened as he slowly lowered his chin. Ralph followed the instructions in a mindful way. When his chin was about level, he stood quietly for a minute or so with his hands at his sides, and then began rubbing his thumbs and fingers together. In order to help him penetrate his experience, the trainer asked him if his fingers were rubbing his

his thumbs were rubbing his fingers. This

t him deep in his experience for twenty-five

seconds or so. The answer was not so important as the effect of the question of keeping him tuned to his immediate experience as the only source for finding the answer. He remained focused and receptive to his hands longer than he might have if he had not been questioned. Instead of remarking on them, speculating about them, or explaining them, he simply stayed with the actual experience and studied it more carefully.

When Ralph replied that his fingers were rubbing his thumbs, the trainer proposed an experiment of doing it for him, of taking over what he was already doing for himself. He agreed. He observed his inner reactions as the trainer started to stroke his thumbs. After about ten seconds Ralph went from a calm, studious demeanor to sudden, deep sobbing and collapsed in the trainer's arms. By rubbing his thumbs with his fingers Ralph had been unconsciously saying something reassuring to himself like, "You're okay. You are just as important as these others." He had been reinforcing this belief by holding his head up and back, which of course did not provide him with the assurance and inclusion he sought. In fact, it generally worked against him because it gave people the impression that he did not want contact and it sometimes made them feel intimidated. When the trainer took over this mechanism for him, it was as though someone else was repeating the words he had been longing to hear but never expected anyone else to say. He was receiving directly what he had been searching for unconsciously and indirectly for so many years.

Ralph's session was a good example of how the body, the voluntary musculature, is controlled by and reveals mental life, and how touch and bodily interventions can speak directly to the unconscious. When we value our bodies and listen to them more closely, we become more connected to ourselves and to the world around us.

TRUSTING

信

Who can wait quietly while the
mud settles?
Who can remain still until the moment
of action?
(Feng & English, 15)

Lao Tzu believed that in addition to being subtle, mysterious, competent, and responsive, the ancient masters were characterized by patience. They would remain unmoving until the right action became apparent. Therapy requires good timing. Timing is inevitably ruined when the therapist feels a need to fill in space, to do something just to produce more visible action. If we are mindfully exploring some issue, it can be like giving birth. The mother and the midwife know significant things are happening, but someone peeking into the room once in a while might not pick this up. "Nothing happening yet. No birth." The art is to sense when something organic should be

trusted, and when something has become disconnected from the thread and needs attention. When something is developing organically, the next right action inevitably suggests itself, as does the right rhythm for acting. Much of therapy is an act of trust. When things seem muddy, we can be patient if we believe they will eventually become clear.

> *When trust is insufficient, there will be no trust in return.*
> *(Henricks, 17)*

> *Governing a large country*
> *is like frying a small fish.*
> *You spoil it with too much poking.*
> *(Mitchell, 60)*

Gus was part of a new training group studying psychotherapy. At the beginning of a daily session when it was his turn to speak, Gus began discussing his trouble with people in authority. He spoke for five minutes or so and became quite emotional. He described problems and indicated ways the trainer could intervene to "work" with him. The trainer did not feel ready to do that. She sensed Gus's desperation, frustration, and fear—all of which had led Gus to remain trapped by continuous ruminations about what was causing his trouble and how he might obtain relief. To accept Gus's invitation to intervene at this point would add to his turbulence and reinforce his preoccupation with his pain.

While Gus spoke, the birds outside occasionally poured out their own songs. The trainer thought of helping him realize the wonderful richness that he was missing by being wrapped up in his thoughts, but Gus was speaking and she felt it would be disruptive to intervene. As the trainer remained patient a suitable moment emerged. Gus had in some way said all there was to say and had begun to repeat himself. A seagull screeched and a couple of seconds later the trainer said softly, "Did you hear the seagull?" Gus stopped, clutched his chest, and burst into tears. Upon hearing the question, he explained later, he had felt a great emotional pain in his heart at being lost, isolated, and not in touch with the world around him. He also felt a joyful quality of grief at being reunited with the sounds, sights, and smells that could nourish him whenever he was receptive to them.

Waiting for the right moment, not chasing each opportunity, using the simple things around that fit effortlessly into the process, allowing Gus to be the focus of his own meditation, were all expressions of nondoing and patience on the part of the trainer.

SEEKING TRUTH

When there is no peace within the family,
Filial piety and devotion arise.
When the country is confused and in chaos,
Loyal ministers appear.
(Feng & English, 18)

Lao Tzu was a penetrating critic of conventional morality. As with Freud after him, he knew that outward virtues could mask inner opposites. Laws on top of laws are legislated to cover loopholes when the heart is not in right relationship.

Therapy sessions can be ruled and ruined by conventional morality when there is not a willingness and an ability to be instructed by what is. The rules governing normal conversation can take over, overriding the unconventional practice of speaking from a mindful place. Being proper can prevent being spontaneous.

As clients, a part of us wants to please the therapist, and will be good, too good, about going along with whatever the therapist's agenda is. Assuming that therapists generally want to be pleased and appreciated as opposed to challenged or criticized, we will often take on the job of protecting them. Mutual collusion and accommodation may keep the therapy process unending and unreal for years on end. In this way our character is reinforced, rather than transcended.

Eugene Gendlin, who works at the University of Chicago, has done a great deal of research on what makes a successful therapy client. He concludes that it has more to do with bodily intelligence than with cleverness and knowledge. When we can give up the convention of knowing for simply experiencing, therapy progresses. Gendlin listens to therapy tapes to hear whether we, as clients, come up with experiential answers to therapeutic inquiries. If we do not, he predicts that the therapy will remain at the level of already conscious intellectual activity, even over a long period of time. Therapists can facilitate a transformative process that helps open us to new possibilities by staying with questions that direct us into our bodily experience as opposed to our theories. To respond to a question such as "Which one of your ears is slightly warmer than the other?" requires a radically different kind of inquiry from the question "*Why* is one of your ears warmer than the other?" In his classes on the Focusing Method, Gendlin teaches ways in which people can concentrate on the alive, *felt sense* of an issue as opposed to wandering off into disembodied theories *about* the issue. Although experiential, bodily knowledge can be frightening because it is so radically raw and uncontained by our theories, Lao Tzu cautions against exchanging it for the conventional wisdom of abstractions which place a veneer over truth.

> *When the great Tao is forgotten,*
> *Kindness and morality arise.*
> *When wisdom and intelligence are born,*
> *The great pretence begins.*
> *(Feng & English, 18)*

AFFIRMING CREATION

Abandon sageliness and discard wisdom;
Then the people will benefit a hundredfold.
(Chan, 19)

Taoism is a radical affirmation of the trust-worthiness of creation. It takes precedence even over the wisdom we seek, because wisdom itself can be made into an idol, perverted and objectified in a way that fosters great harm. Whenever we think we have something we can clutch or grasp in certainty, there is danger. All spiritual traditions undercut our attachments and allegiances that we lean on for security, for these are the very things that lead us to defend, impose, and attack.

In another chapter Lao Tzu says

Thus, Tao is great,
Heaven is great, earth is great, and man is great
too.
In the universe we have four greatnesses.
(Chang, 25)

Living and resting in the life we are given supports simplicity, understanding, satisfaction, and peace. By contrast, being clever, setting up codes of ethics, judging right and wrong, and making either/or decisions inevitably sets up dichotomy. Creation becomes divided against itself. Barriers are erected to the organic unfolding of what is needed.

The general wisdom of the psychotherapeutic community is not immune from these cautions against rigidified knowledge. Jung-Yuan walked into a mental health center claiming he was weak, unable to function well in his work life, filled with longing, and needing what he had never received. Alarm bells went off in the staff. "No, this person's judgment cannot be trusted. This is an oral personality who can suck a therapist dry." A confrontation quickly ensued. In a second evaluation interview the counselor tried to tell Jung-Yuan, "No, you are not needy. You can never recover what you missed in your childhood. You have what it takes. You need to get in touch with your strength and independence. You do not need more than one appointment a week or my home phone number."

Jung-Yuan left the mental health center feeling even more defeated, with a slight sense of anger, but with little motivation to go back. A friend referred him to someone in private practice who had a more nonviolent approach that led to a different response and result. The therapist did not attempt to discount Jung-Yuan's neediness, but supported it while suggesting that he be mindful in the process. Jung-Yuan discovered a part of himself that was afraid to let in the nourishment the therapist was making available. He was invited to explore this barrier to letting in good things. He then became a witness to his fears which automatically defended against nourishment (the very thing he thought he was ready, able, and wanting to take in). Later he discovered a willingness to let in nourishment on a qualified basis; a basis that acknowledged his fears that it might be soon taken away, or that it might be erratic and unpredictable. After consciously accepting support from the therapist and allowing it to nourish him for a while, Jung-Yuan noticed another need come into his awareness—that of wanting to be independent and stand on his own. Eventually, the conflict between being needy and being independent was transcended. Jung-Yuan realized it was an illusory choice. He could both be supported *and* take care of business by himself. He could both be supported *and* support others.

During this process of affirming the neediness instead of fighting it, the therapist gave Jung-Yuan his home phone number and agreed to see him three times a week for the first three weeks, after which they would both reevaluate the number of sessions needed, a foolish thing to do by the standards of those who understand therapy as a kind of power struggle. This therapist, however, had trusted that there was wisdom in Jung-Yuan's experience (perverted and unrealistic as it may have appeared on the surface), that closely following and respecting his experience would lead to an understandable inner core, and that finally there would be simple needs which could be realistically addressed. Luckily, he was not working according to therapeutic lore which said he would be drained and overwhelmed if he accommodated Jung-Yuan's expressed needs and wishes.

Still, it is hard to have faith when someone seems un-balanced and irrational, even though metabolic factors have been ruled out. It is hard not to invoke and impose rationally correct, ideal solutions born of accumulated sageness. It is good to have the affirmation of Lao Tzu who does not have our reticence about shedding conventional wisdom.

Drop humanity, abandon justice,
And the people will return to their natural affections.
(Wu, 19)

CLAIMING

If you want to become whole,
let yourself be partial.
If you want to become straight,
let yourself be crooked.
(Mitchell, 22)

Here is a nice statement of what Gestalt therapy would later label the paradoxical theory of change. We move beyond our present situation by claiming it. If we come into a therapist's office presenting as a problem the need to be something different, and the therapist accepts the same view and offers help, the whole process is over before it begins. James Hillman, the Jungian therapist, once expressed it by saying we do not have problems: we *are* problems. The solution can never be the riddance of the problem; it can only be the care that leads to an affirmation of trust in ourselves and the creation.

Jungian therapists in general talk about the "shadow"—the side of ourselves we fear, dislike, and keep out of conscious awareness—and the "persona"—the side we accept, are proud of, and allow into our consciousness. Healing, as the *Tao-te ching* clearly indicates, does not come from increasing the amount of light in our lives, but from reaching into the shadow and drawing unreconciled elements of ourselves into the light where they can be healed.

Exploring the pain attached to our shadows in therapy is not promoting pain for its own sake. Rather, pain becomes the clue for leading us to what needs healing, which in turn leads to greater wholeness of self and communion with the rest of creation. Those of us who feel deprived learn to recognize and integrate our independence and power. Those of us who use these qualities to excess learn to be comfortable with intimacy and vulnerability. Those who shy away from contact with people learn to leave the safety of isolation and deal with issues in the company of others. Those who under stress turn to people, learn to cultivate their aloneness and inner strength.

In this process of healing and growing we do not completely disown or leave behind old ways of relating to the world. It is simply that new ways of relating are added to our repertoire, and a measure of awareness and choice is introduced where before we acted habitually and automatically. None of this happens, however, by denying or avoiding our

present way of being. We must acknowledge and take responsibility for who we are now in order for new horizons to
open up.

> *If you want to become full,*
> *let yourself be empty.*
> *If you want to be reborn,*
> *let yourself die.*
> *(Mitchell, 22)*

OBSERVING NATURE

自然

Man models himself after Earth.
Earth models itself after Heaven.
Heaven models itself after Tao.
And Tao models itself after Nature.
(Chan, 25)

The *Tao-te ching* suggests that nature is the best model for everything, perhaps especially for psychotherapy. Indeed, the current study of living systems theory and sciences of complexity yields a rich resource that offers a more inclusive paradigm than the mechanical, medical model flowing from the Newtonian worldview. The philosopher-anthropologist Gregory Bateson, for instance, talked about characteristics of a living organic system. It is a whole made up of parts. What makes it organic is that the parts communicate within the whole. When they do, the organism is self-directing, self-correcting, and characterized by a complex and essential unpredictability. We cannot

say that a particular input will determine a definite outcome or specified response because a living organic system has a mind of its own. The wisdom is within. It is not run by authority from without. It takes whatever comes to it from without and processes it in complex ways before it decides what it has experienced and how it will express itself in response. The amount of energy it has is of less importance than how information is processed to use that energy. A human mind can organize a small amount of energy to accomplish incredible feats, such as going to the moon, while a raging rhinoceros expends a great deal of energy without being able to organize it to accomplish anything very creative.

Mindful, nonviolent psychotherapy can be thought of as an enterprise that studies *the organization of experience.* How do we organize experience and expression in our lives, automatically, without even thinking about it? What fears arise when we contemplate organizing in a new way? How can those fears be allayed so that reorganization can take place?

If a therapist asks a group of us to be mindful, slow down, and turn our awareness inward to simply witness whatever reactions we have when he says the words "You are a good person," the experiment will yield different responses in each of us. This is because we each organize our experience differently. Some of us may accept the notion.

Some may reject it in one way or another. Some may feel nothing, others happiness or tears. Each of us filters and interprets each moment of existence differently. When therapists propose these little experiments in awareness in a mindful state of consciousness, they are helping us study our habits of organizing, our dispositions and assumptions, our manner of perceiving, and our style of taking action, all of which can lead us to our deepest beliefs. It is through discovering these long-held ideas which organize so much of our perception and action that we can begin to modify them. It is awe-inspiring to consider that of all nature's children, we human beings are the only ones we know of who can become self-conscious about our beliefs and transform our lives by incorporating new ones more in harmony with the Tao while never forgetting that we always remain within the Tao.

CENTERING

*Though there are beautiful things to
be seen,
He remains unattached and calm.
(Feng & English, 26)*

The Taoist sage knows that beauty and drama can be invitations to distraction and
restlessness as well as being intrinsically
edifying. The wise one stays in touch with
both her roots and her direction while
traveling through glorious vistas. In therapy, rising and falling emotions provide an
analogy with the magnificent landscapes Lao
Tzu mentions. Strong emotion can be the
occasion for getting lost in therapy. It can
sometimes frighten therapists and overpower them, so that they communicate a
verbal or nonverbal message to us to tone it
down. Conversely, emotion can seem so
rich and full that therapists become fascin-
ated with it for its own sake. They can be
involved in trying to promote it subtly even

though it is not organically wanting to unfold. Intense, *spontaneous* emotion need only be supported. If our back arches, a therapist can brace the arch with a hand and matching pressure. If we begin to curl up, therapists can help us to do that. Riding the emotional rapids in this manner is not an optimal time for us to be mindful. We are probably too busy releasing tears and emotion, while also trying to contain them through restricted breathing and the muscular tensing of all or part of our bodies. It is chaotic and noisy, although precisely what is necessary. The therapist does not invite us to be reflective, but simply stays with us, providing safety through buttressing what is, until the storm is over and there is once again a place for the witness. Strong emotion is neither promoted nor discouraged, but naturally supported when it arises as an organic part of the process.

Therapists can also be blown to and fro by chasing every sensation, feeling, memory, and thought that we report. It is a therapeutic art to know when the shifts from thoughts to sensation to feeling to memory to meaning are connected by the same thread, and when they are diversions from it. Whenever either we and/or the therapist become bored and restless, it is a good clue that the thread has been abandoned and something needs to be done to regain perspective and return to what is wanting to happen. Sometimes it is helpful for either us or the therapist to do a little housekeeping by observing that it feels as though the process is no longer connected to its root threads, and talking a little about what is necessary to get back in touch.

> *If you let yourself be blown to and fro,*
> *you lose touch with your root.*
> *If you let restlessness move you,*
> *you lose touch with who you are.*
> *(Mitchell, 26)*

WANDERING

A good traveler has no fixed plans
and is not intent upon arriving.
A good artist lets his intuition
lead him wherever it wants.
A good scientist has freed himself of concepts
and keeps his mind open to what is. . . .

He is ready to use all situations
and doesn't waste anything.
(Mitchell, 27)

This is called "following the light."
(Feng & English, 27)

Chapter 27 of the *Tao-te ching* suggests that those who are best at what they do are not bound by the axioms, rules, and limits of their fields, but allow themselves to be directed by their open, intuitive imaginations. This does not suggest, however, that they have not primed their minds by studying widely and deeply.

Similarly, experienced psychotherapists should have a wealth of theoretical and experiential background knowledge to draw on when they explore our predicaments and hopes with us. Material we touch on gives them hunches about what is going on and the direction things may go in. However, this knowledge must work in the background. Following and responding to our moment-to-moment experience must be a priority. Although there is a spoken or unspoken agreement with us that a pilgrimage is under way, no fixed plans, structures, or theories should be imposed on the wandering in the wilderness.

The Master gives himself up
to whatever the moment brings.
(Mitchell, 50)

Intuition and inventiveness true to the principles of the Tao are what make a good guide. An ancient Chinese proverb says that the way is easy for those who have no preferences. No matter how much therapists know, they need to work with no preferences for proving or imposing what they know. This stance allows new possibilities and learning to emerge for both them and us. The British Object Relations therapist D. W. Winnicott once said that it does not matter how much therapists know, as long as they can keep it to themselves, and allow us to discover what is true to our own reality. The best leader follows, just as the greatest master serves.

Milton Erickson, the American medical hypnotist, was one guide who was ready to use all situations and did not waste anything. His "utilization techniques," which employed whatever clients put forth, are justly famous and instructive. When a patient in a hospital ward introduced himself as Jesus Christ, Erickson did not argue with him, but responded with, "Oh, I understand you have experience as a carpenter, yes? Here, let me show you the shop. We have some good woodworking tools you can get into." He accepted the person's experience of reality, quieted the storm raging around him, and got him reconnected to the earth where spontaneous reorganization had a chance to work its miracles. When he first went to meet this man, Erickson did not have fixed plans. His response was not a technique he learned in medical school, though it was informed by a profound knowledge of human nature. It was simply one that felt appropriate to the situation.

> *Supple like a tree in the wind,*
> *he has no destination in view*
> *and makes use of anything*
> *life happens to bring his way.*
> *(Mitchell, 59)*

When we enter into therapy with an experienced guide we never know where we will end up, and would do well to both expect and affirm that. Marci started out in therapy because she was depressed at not getting a scholarship to study social work, and she could not motivate herself to do anything else. She giggled as she discussed this. When the therapist invited her to explore her giggling, she eventually recalled that she had always wanted to build boats with her uncle in the San Juan Islands, although she knew that that would probably disappoint her parents. She began to distinguish what she herself wanted from what others wanted for her. Her willingness to wander from the narrow concern for her depression to explore a seemingly unrelated giggle led her to a central concern she had been unaware of.

> In caring for others and serving heaven,
> There is nothing like using restraint.
> Restraint begins with giving up one's own ideas.
> This depends on Virtue gathered in the past.
> If there is a good store of Virtue, then nothing is impossible.
> (Feng & English, 59)

RESTORING THE CHILD

归於樸

If you are a pattern for the world,
the Tao will be strong inside you
and there will be nothing you can't do. . . .

If you accept the world,
the Tao will be inside you
and you will return to your primal self.
(Mitchell, 28)

Sanity, for Lao Tzu, is accepting the creation just as it is.

Do you think you can take over the universe
and improve it?
I do not believe it can be done.

The universe is sacred.
You cannot improve it.
If you try to change it, you will ruin it.
If you try to hold it, you will lose it.
(Feng & English, 29)

Sanity is crucial for our safety as clients. If we feel that therapists have judgments about us or have agendas for making us more accept-able, we will close down, become defensive, and the process will go nowhere. We sense whether therapists believe that the world, themselves, and we are worthwhile. Their atti-tude communicates whether they know there is a forgiveness and grace in the universe which does not require perfection on their part or ours.

When a therapist's sanity encourages us to accept more of life, often a frightened inner child is evoked who decided long ago that some things were unacceptable. A state of consciousness arises in which we are both aware of being an adult in therapy, and becoming that inner child in thought, speech, memory, mannerisms, and belief. In this state, be-liefs that we adopted as children come to the surface and new, more nourishing beliefs can be explored and integrated with them. When more life is received, more of the inner child can live in harmony with previously alienated aspects of our-selves and the world around us. We come closer to our primal selves.

> To find the origin,
> trace back the manifestations.
> When you recognize the children
> and find the mother, you will be free. . . .
> (Mitchell, 52)

One who is steeped in Virtue is akin to the new-born babe. . . .
Growing in its wholeness, and keeping its vitality in its perfect
integrity.
It howls and screams all day long without getting hoarse,
Because it embodies perfect harmony. . . .

To hasten the growth of life is ominous.
To control the breath by the will is to overstrain it.
(Wu, 55)

Melinda entered therapy because her relationships were confused and unsatisfactory. She was very social as well as highly competent and physically attractive. She could meet people easily, entertain them with grace and laughter, and dramatize any routine occurrence as if it were a truly marvelous event in the history of humankind. People liked her and were drawn to her, but she was still unhappy. She would often become depressed, although she maintained a vibrant exterior. She had a vague sense of being angry that people did not love her fully. There always seemed to be something missing for her.

The therapeutic process eventually led back to the time when Melinda was three and her aunt Susan was living with her and her parents. Her beloved aunt had delighted in Melinda and spent many mutually enjoyable hours with her before marrying and moving out of state. Melinda's parents had been happy to have Susan spend so much time with her, since they were both busy people with limited energy. When Susan left, Melinda's parents felt the burden of looking after an active, social child and tended to ignore her until Melinda threw some kind of tantrum. They would then deal with her in a harsh and negative way.

Little Melinda had been bewildered. She knew something was wrong, and concluded that it must be she who was at fault. Probably she was not interesting enough for adults to pay attention to her and include her in their activities. She began to raise the volume of her voice in order to be heard and transformed even little things into dramatic events. She also noted carefully those things her parents liked or did not like and then behaved in a way calculated to receive the most response. This entire process was not so much logical and conscious as experimental, haphazard, and unreflective.

On one level Melinda was quite successful with both her parents and others around her, as she grew too quickly into adult company. On another level, she could never relinquish the longing to be effortlessly delighted in. Little Melinda was sad and angry because she felt she had to bolster her energy artificially and shine in order to be included. She was lonely as she grew and developed since she was constantly presenting a false front to people. Even when she moved beyond the confines of her early family environment, she never learned that she could reassess her situation and discover that there were now people in her life who were willing to hear and acknowledge her without requiring a performance. She no longer needed to turn up the volume or seduce everyone into paying attention to her. Her life began to change as Little Melinda, the inner child, entered into communication with Grown Melinda. Both began to understand what had happened. Most important, they began to let in new experiences of acceptance, although the experience of simply being Melinda without the extra drama was frightening at first.

Bioenergetic therapist Alexander Lowen explains the freight of Melinda and others by saying that the main task for all of us in therapy is to learn how to tolerate pleasure. Even though we want pleasure, it is hard to allow it when we are anxious and fearful about being disappointed or hurt as we were when we were children. In the end, the needs of the inner child are simple and straightforward, even in situations where there has been pain. When the confusion, hurt, and wants of the inner child are acknowledged and related to in a compassionate, realistic way, we are much more ready to accept life and be ourselves.

> *Be the stream of the universe!*
> *Being the stream of the universe,*
> *Ever true and unswerving,*
> *Become as a little child once more.*
> *(Feng & English, 28)*

RELINQUISHING CONTROL

勿強

The Master does his job
and then stops.
He understands that the universe
is forever out of control,
and that trying to dominate events
goes against the current of the Tao.
(Mitchell, 30)

Another prerequisite for good therapists is being comfortable with not being in control. The whole process depends on using the spontaneous as a beginning and continuing point of departure. To do this requires the ability to give up not only personal agendas (see the chapter on "Communing," earlier), but also therapeutic agendas.

In a group setting the therapist suggested to Karen, "Notice what happens to your shoulders when Tim moves slightly closer to you." Immediately, before the experiment was even set up, Karen's foot started to move. That became the spontaneous. The experiment was put on hold temporarily, possibly permanently. "So just this suggestion causes your foot to move, huh?" When Karen became aware of the movement of her foot, she developed a strange taste in her mouth. The spontaneous shifted to another physical reaction.

The process started with Karen's noticing a slight upward movement of her shoulders whenever she joined a group or when another group member arrived and sat close to her. What did moving feet and strange tastes mean? The therapist had no idea. She and Karen were wandering in a mysterious darkness with a dynamic of its own. This was a place where therapy was an act of trust for the therapist. She knew only that trying to control or impose some order on what was unfolding, or stopping to analyze what was happening, would prevent it from leading Karen to where she needed to go. So the therapist assumed that the best leader follows, and paid respectful attention to Karen's observation. She asked a question whose answer made no difference, except that it encouraged Karen to remain with her experience: "Is the taste bitter or sour?" Trusting the universe to lead the way home, encouraging mindful awareness, the therapist just did her job. This trust was rewarded when Karen brought to awareness an old memory of being sexually abused. This memory made sense out of the whole chain of connections. Noninterference yielded what controlling forcefulness could rarely, if ever, achieve, and it did so in record time. Nondoing yields great utility.

> *Trying to control the future*
> *is like trying to take the master carpenter's place.*
> *When you handle the master carpenter's tools,*
> *chances are that you'll cut your hand.*
> *(Mitchell, 74)*

DEALING WITH ENEMIES

Fine weapons of war augur evil.
Even things seem to hate them.
Therefore, a man of Tao does not set his
heart upon them. . . .

As weapons are instruments of evil,
They are not properly a gentleman's in-
struments;
Only of necessity will he resort to them.
For peace and quiet are dearest to his heart,
And to him even a victory is no cause
for rejoicing.
(Wu, 31)

His enemies are not demons,
but human beings like himself.
He doesn't wish them personal harm. . . .

He enters a battle gravely,
with sorrow and with great compassion.
(Mitchell, 31)

The Taoist sage is a person of peace who does not consider his enemies to be less human than he is. He considers the use of weapons tragic. However, he will resort to them if necessary. While a country that is at one with the Tao will produce tractors instead of tanks, Lao Tzu does not suggest the abolition of all police forces.

> *Patient with both friends and enemies,*
> *you accord with the ways things are.*
> *(Mitchell, 67)*

> *Mercy alone can help you to win a war. . . .*
> *For Heaven will come to the rescue of the merciful, and protect*
> *him with* its *Mercy.*
> *(Wu, 67)*

> *To engage in war lightly is to violate my essential teachings of*
> *compassion, renunciation, and never longing to be first in the*
> *world.*
> *Therefore, when two armies join in battle,*
> *The one that is compassionate wins.*
> *(Chang, 69)*

Seeking therapy assumes we are willing to become mindful and explore our inner world. It assumes we have a sense of responsibility for our world and our actions, and a willingness to claim our part in what is happening in our lives. What about those who have been labeled as having personality disorders, because they project blame for their situation on everything and everybody other than themselves? What about those labeled antisocial because they may push an old lady into oncoming traffic if she refuses to let go of her purse, and not give it another thought? What about spouse-beaters, child-molesters, and substance-abusers who endanger other lives to feed their habits?

People acting out these disorders can be thought of as enemies of the Tao. They are doing destructive, hurtful things to innocent people. They would not ordinarily volunteer for therapy, but must be related to, both for the well-being of the community and also for their own well-being. Forceful tools must often be brought to bear even to have them consider therapeutic work: the reality of lost jobs, lost relationships, or incarceration. It is not a loving thing to allow people to continue living in their illusions and not encounter the consequences of their actions.

Who is best qualified to bring forceful tools to bear? Lao Tzu suggests those who have sorrow and great compassion. Their sorrow is the ability to feel the pain of those who have been hurt. Their compassion is the ability to identify with the one who has done the hurting, to know that they are more like the hurtful one than different.

The Tao is the hidden Reservoir of all things.
A treasure to the honest, it is a safeguard to the erring.
(Wu, 62)

It is difficult for therapists to help a rapist or racist if they have not made peace with the rapist or racist within themselves. If they do not do this first, their use of power will give rise to defenses against power in the offender, who will avoid change by playing whatever game is necessary to maintain the status quo. Therapists who recognize their own ability to manipulate, and who can employ power efficiently and dispassionately, are those with the best chance of transcending the manipulation and power plays of the offender. Therapists who can be honest and straightforward, communicating a sense of common human-beingness, are the ones who have the best chance of inviting offenders into the self-awareness of therapeutic processes.

When Tao prevails in the world, evil loses its power.
It is not that evil no longer possesses spiritual power.
It is that its power does not damage men.
Indeed, it is not that its power does not damage men.
It is primarily that the ruler does not become harmful to men.
When opposites no longer damage each other,
Both are benefitted through the attainment of Tao.
(Chang, 60)

Although the techniques employed for working with willing and unwilling persons may look radically different, the same underlying principles of the Tao apply.

> *"To the good I am good;*
> *to the non-good I am also good,*
> *for Life is goodness.*
> *To the faithful I am faithful;*
> *to the unfaithful I am also faithful,*
> *for Life is faithfulness." . . .*
> *the Man of Calling accepts them all as his children.*
> *(Wilhelm, 49)*

ADJUSTING

Tao in the world is like a river flowing
home to the sea.
(Feng & English, 32)

The image Lao Tzu offers of rivers flowing to their destinations calms anxiety. We do not have to worry about whether a river goes north, south, straight, or takes innumerable twists and turns. The river will eventually find its home in the sea. In therapeutic processes there is a great deal of forgiveness and opportunity for a variety of approaches. This is no surprise when we remember that everything originates in the  Tao and is connected to everything else in creation. If some people claim that we can begin to understand ourselves by looking at our relationships, others point to body structure and movement, and still others examine eyes, feet, diet, or something else, do we have to make a choice? No. That would be either/or thinking that posits only one right answer and a host of wrong ones. There is room here for everybody to be right, if each person is a careful observer of human experience.

Does a therapist need to discover the best method to reach our core beliefs right from the start in order for mindfulness to lead us home? No. All roads lead home. All rivers flow down to the sea. Theoretically, a therapist could start with any psychological aspect of our lives, and this would lead back to whatever in us is organizing it: a sensation or feeling, a habitual gesture, a facial expression, a way of standing, the kind of clothes we wear, the way we say "hello," and so on. The emergency emerges, as Gestalt therapist Fritz Perls once remarked.

There is therapeutic art, of course. It has to do with sensing where the chronic, unchanging, unconscious aspects of our character manifest, where the energy is, and with being able to evoke those aspects within us so that we can explore them more consciously and deeply. But if one experiment is not quite on target, it will soon become apparent and the process will correct itself, because we are organic systems whose inner wisdom can be trusted. Good therapists are always watching for visual clues and consulting with us to see whether our own experience confirms the direction in which the process is moving.

An example: Jesse was in a group for Vietnam veterans.

One night he spoke about feeling a need to take on the leadership of a community organization, but not being able to bring himself to do it, although the cause was important and he had the necessary skills. It felt as if some force were preventing him.

As Jesse spoke his body was leaning slightly forward, as if pushing against an invisible force or leaning into the wind. So, the therapist decided to physicalize the issue by placing his hand in the middle of Jesse's chest, approximating the pressure of the opposing force, and saying "No!" out loud. Jesse observed his own reactions to this experiment, and as the process deepened, his emotions became stronger, and he realized that part of him was frustrated, wanting to take on leadership, and help something to happen. He also felt as if he were being held back (at the same time as being opposed), so a couple of other veterans held back his arms in a way that Jesse directed. It was an exercise in taking over, of doing for Jesse what he had been doing for himself, and this had the effect of calming the muscular tension in him, so that he could become more sensitive to hearing the inner signals of his mind.

To the therapist, who had not been to Vietnam, Jesse looked as though he were manifesting a classic case of a rigid or conscientious character process. A person disposed to conscientiousness is often frustrated at not being included, still feeling a childhood need to perform to show that he is as good as everyone else. The child may feel a need to prove his worth by making the team or getting the good grade in order to get a parent's love and attention. Assuming some such dynamic to be at work, the therapist asked Jessie to watch what happened when the therapist said things like, "You can take charge. We're on your side. You don't have to prove anything to us." Jesse did not have any particular reaction to any of these verbal experiments. Then one of the other veterans whispered in his ear, "But someone might get killed," and Jessie immediately collapsed in tears. As his brothers held him, memories of Vietnam flooded over him; life-and-death situations in which his decisions had literally resulted in death for others. He allowed repressed aspects of his experience into consciousness, and grieved. He eventually sorted through what it meant that the war was over, and how the meaning of his leadership in the present was both the same as and different from what it had been during the war.

Here is a good example of how group wisdom can bring correction to a situation. It also exemplifies how later experiences in our lives can take precedence over early developmental issues that therapists often have in mind. In addition it demonstrates how there is forgiveness in a process. The therapist proceeded experimentally, without attachment to his hunch, and was willing to let go of his direction when it

did not prove fruitful. Room was allowed for other intuitions, and the process ended up going where it needed
to go.

> *Why did the ancients prize the Tao?*
> *Is it not because by virtue of it he who seeks finds,*
> *And the guilty are forgiven?*
> *That is why it is such a treasure to the world.*
> *(Wu, 62)*

SIMPLY BEING

He who knows men is clever;
He who knows himself has insight.
He who conquers men has force;
He who conquers himself is truly strong.

He who knows when he has got enough
is rich. . . .
And he who dies but perishes not enjoys
real longevity.
(Wu, 33)

The principles of nonviolent, nondoing, mindful therapy are fundamental. If the therapist lives and breathes them, techniques evolve naturally as the process goes along. If the therapist is not grounded personally and professionally in the principles, the techniques simply will not work. The therapist is her own best instrument.

When a superior man hears of the Tao,
he immediately begins to embody it.
(Mitchell, 41)

He doesn't think about his actions;
they flow from the core of his being.
(Mitchell, 50)

One of the reasons the therapist is able to accept us in our world, is that she herself enjoys and is nourished by the world as it is. She is rich. She realizes that she has enough, and embodies that realization. She lives this affirmation of trust, which is what gives her work integrity.

The sage knows without going about,
Understands without seeing.
(Chan, 47)

Being content with what she has means she is at peace with her own limitations. She can stay in the center. She is no longer controlled by threats in the form of demands to make people happy and to meet their expectations. She is not governed by the need to control, to be liked, or to validate a client's feelings in an attempt to validate her own.

Although there is a great deal that she does not know and cannot do, she can still be a person of wisdom and true power. We feel, therefore, that we can trust her with ourselves. As clients, we do not have to defend ourselves against her or take care of her. She can yield, making room for us to grow.

Notice that none of this has to do with the therapist

trying to attain illusory standards of perfection. She is trust-worthy, not because she is superior to us, but precisely because she has made peace with her ambiguities and yearn-ings which make her like us. Because she realizes that life is bountiful and graceful with her, as she is, she can often be more gentle with us than we can be with ourselves. In addition, she allows herself to grow and learn more about the ways of peace and trust through being instructed by us in our process as we grow.

> *Be content with what you have;*
> *rejoice in the way things are.*
> *When you realize there is nothing lacking,*
> *the whole world belongs to you.*
> *(Mitchell, 44)*

NOT STRIVING

不自为大

The magnificent Tao is all-pervading. . . .
All creatures abide with it and grow,
none are excluded from it.
When its work is done, it does not de-
mand merit.
It nurtures all things, but does not rule
them. . . .
Therefore, the wise does not endeavor to
be great.
Hence, his attainment is great.
(Chang, 34)

The most powerful thing the therapist does for us is provide a setting, a nourishing womb, in which our lives can unfold. Through the physical setting and, most important, the setting of his own being, he creates a place of safety; a trustworthy place where all of life is befriended through an affirmation of faith in our wisdom and creativity.

Hold fast to the great form (Tao),
And all the world will come.
They come and will encounter no harm;
But enjoy comfort, peace, and health.
(Chan, 35)

When the setting is right, the work, the inner explorations, happen by themselves. The unity of the Tao moves to overcome separations and make parts into wholes. Our process often develops with minimal need for guidance. The master therapist is always noted for how little he does. He helps us realize how we have empowered ourselves, how our growth and change is of our own doing. He gives perfect freedom for inner wisdom to lead us where we need to go, even if that means away from him.

He also realizes that though the power of the Tao is available in his therapeutic setting and within us to do whatever needs to be done through nondoing, we might not recognize this. That is the reason we have come to him. We do not quite have eyes to see and ears to hear. We are often controlled by unconscious fears and need a grace-full presence to be with us as we face those fears. So, he is patient. He works on safety first, knowing that it is always defined through *our perception* of it, rational or otherwise. At this beginning stage, he looks as if he were doing more, responding more, than at transformative stages where nondoing is more easily embraced and trusted.

Since he provides this setting with such ease, he is often surprised by the expressions of gratitude he receives. On one level, the gratitude is appropriate. It is a rare gift to find someone who can help by not being too helpful, who can facilitate without getting in the way, who can be involved without mixing up his own needs with ours, and who can be a midwife for transformation without taking credit away from the mother and child. Still, his helpful ways stem from paying attention to his own need for sanity and enjoyment of life, letting the Tao do what it does best, and not trying to make anything special happen. He can claim no credit for satisfactory outcomes. He is thankful for this, since it means he has no reputation to uphold or defend. It is simply wonderful in itself to be present when a child is given birth. It is inherently marvelous to behold a wounded child relinquish its fear and receive what it thought was impossible.

The sage never strives for the great,
And thereby the great is achieved.
(Chan, 63)

JUMPING

The Master views the parts with compassion,
because he understands the whole.
(Mitchell, 39)

As mentioned earlier, it is possible to lose one's way in therapy. Therapists can become overwhelmed by the turns, twists, and details of our story and drawn down into the sheer impossibility of any satisfying solution. They can get caught with us in self-perpetuating games which prevent the process from deepening. They may chase us for information and the harder they chase, the faster we run. We may respond to their questions by giving answers and waiting passively for the next question. We may free-associate for years without ever touching what is important. They may follow our experience all over the map from headaches, to sensations in the stomach, dreams, pains in the heel, and concerns about attire, yet still nothing deepens in an organic way. Many articles have been written about the self-perpetuating systems in which therapists and clients can get trapped and which result in interminable and unsatisfying therapy.

Therapists have to be able to go back and forth from being intimately connected to the fine grain of what is happening, to being able to stand back and see the whole picture. When they gain a perspective, they may well see that they need to escape from a particular system.

Many dead ends are solved by jumping to a higher-level system that includes the earlier system. One therapist noticed that Ramos reluctantly went along with his suggestions, but that the process foundered every time. The process was very subtle, because Ramos carefully concealed his reluctance. By calling attention to the system through describing it in a curious, nonjudgmental way, the therapist helped Ramos discover a part of himself that was afraid he would not be liked if he did not go along with other people's suggestions. He then became aware of a part of himself that was angry about this feeling of conditional friendship or love, while being afraid to express it. Jumping out of the system (of the therapist making suggestions and Ramos reluctantly following them) eventually led Ramos to an inner child that was loved, but whose self-assertion was squashed, a child who decided he could have closeness only if he gave up the freedom to be who he was. The therapeutic process then regained its live, organic character.

Compassion flows naturally from realizing how one part fits into the whole. For instance, it can be boring and frustrating for therapist and client to follow an unending assortment of aches, symptoms, interesting happenings, evocative associations, and more, as one therapist did with Greta. When a jump to a higher level revealed that Greta was terrified of being ignored, unconsciously angry at not being interesting enough to be included without constantly performing, and desperately trying to get the therapist not to abandon her, the purpose of the stream of symptoms was understood. New options became possible for satisfying her deep need to be included and acknowledged.

In general, the jumps made in therapy that enable us to transcend our self-perpetuating systems are from context to form, statement to assumption, surface manifestation to experiential base, experience to meaning, what is being done to who is doing it and how, thought to thinker, piece to pattern, and expression of character to core. Again, it is important that the therapist and client observe the world, but trust their inner vision. Either one can make the jump, or simply express that something does not seem to be working, that it is time to step back and get a wider perspective on what is happening. Therapy is a mutual collaboration, not a guru-disciple capitulation.

> *Therefore the truly great man dwells on what is real and not*
> *what is on the surface,*
> *On the fruit and not the flower.*
> *(Feng & English, 38)*

WITHDRAWING

What is most perfect seems to be
incomplete. . . .
The greatest skill seems to be clumsy.
The greatest eloquence seems to stutter.
(Chan, 45)

According to Lao Tzu, the best leaders are the ones whom people are least aware of and who promote development in such a way that others say, "We did it ourselves." Good therapy does not draw attention to itself. When a therapist acknowledges some physical reaction, which comes and goes in less than a second, it may emerge from the edges of our consciousness, where it could have been easily ignored, to the center where it can be savored for what it has to teach. "A slight shudder occurs when you think of your brother, doesn't it?" remarked one therapist to Felipe. This observation was made so simply and matter-of-factly that

Felipe paid no special attention to it, but immediately became curious about the shudder.

When the therapist continued by saying, "Maybe the shudder has important information attached to it, if we stay with it a bit. What is the quality of the shudder?" this invitation was clumsily obvious in intent, but with good timing and the right setting it could lead to powerful results. The therapist's skill and sensitivity remained hidden behind simple principles and techniques that were not kept secret from Felipe: believing one awareness will lead organically to another if we allow it, inviting him to slow down and savor his experience more fully.

The meaning of the shudder came to Felipe in a memory of being young, and almost bumping his brother over a cliff because he could not control a large, new bicycle he had received for his birthday. He realized that he had continuously doubted his ability to maintain physical control of his body from that period of his life until the present. When he left the therapy session, he believed quite rightly that he had discovered all this by himself.

[The Master] doesn't glitter like a jewel
but lets himself be shaped by the Tao,
as rugged and common as a stone.
(Mitchell, 39)

Carl Whitaker, a psychiatrist who has been a pioneer in family therapy, sometimes promotes wisdom by saying things that seem so foolish that we can react to them in useful ways. He might have said something like, "Yah, maybe you can't trust yourself to drive anything. Maybe you should get another part-time job, so that you can afford to pay a chauffeur to get you around safely without hurting anything." Here, he would be taking Felipe's self-doubt to the extreme, and Felipe might then react by saying or thinking that the suggestion was ridiculous. "There must be a way to work through my self-doubt so that I can begin to trust my body more fully." In the process of doubting Whitaker, he would begin to take back more control in an area of his life where he had begun to doubt he had any. Whitaker seems not to mind appearing crazy or "rugged and common as a stone" if it helps someone else grow. His responses do not necessarily invite mindfulness. They are offered in the immediacy of face-to-face encounter. However, they create waves in our consciousness that may be helpful to us if we study their contours mindfully.

> *True wisdom seems foolish. . . .*
> *The Master allows things to happen.*
> *She shapes events as they come.*
> *(Mitchell, 45)*

BROADENING HORIZONS

As for your name and your body, which
is the dearer?
As for your body and your wealth, which
is the more to be prized?
As for gain and loss, which is the
more painful?

Thus, an excessive love for anything will
cost you dear in the end.
The storing up of too much goods will entail
a heavy loss.

To know when you have enough is to be
immune from disgrace.
To know when to stop is to be preserved
from perils.
Only thus can you endure long.
(Wu, 44)

Therefore, the contentment one has when
he knows that he has enough, is abiding
contentment indeed.
(Henricks, 46)

These chapters of the *Tao-te ching* help us understand that although we have been talking about therapy in relation to individuals or small groups, it simply embodies principles at work throughout creation.

Lao Tzu's belief in unity—the interdependence and connection of all parts within a greater whole—has significant political-economic ramifications. How would the world look today if seen through the prism of the proper regard for parts within a whole? The capitalist world would clearly be seen as having overemphasized the value of the parts—the autonomous individual—with little regard for the web of life. The communist world would be seen, in contrast, as having distorted emphasis on the whole, with no regard for the integrity, necessity, and nurture of the parts. As of 1990, Japan and Korea (for all their internal troubles and problems) seem to have been most successful in embodying a sense of balance between the needs of management and labor within the context of the needs of a company, the needs of companies within the context of the needs of a nation, and the needs of the nation within the greater context of the world economy.

No matter what political-economic structure we adopt, Lao Tzu predicts problems for any and all who seek happiness in the realms of money, fame, success, and other externals. An embodiment of the Tao reduces needs, and leads to a simplicity that would not support endless consumerism.

If a country is governed wisely. . . .
People enjoy their food,
take pleasure in being with their families,
spend weekends working in their gardens,
delight in the doings of the neighborhood.
(Mitchell, 80)

They are happy in their ways.
Though they live within sight of their neighbors,
And crowing cocks and barking dogs are heard across the way,
Yet they leave each other in peace while they grow old and die.
(Feng & English, 80)

Although the *Tao-te ching* affirms the value of simplicity and being nourished by what is, following the Tao still leads us to attend to the complexity of the needs of the whole, which has tremendous implications for the reorganization of our life together. For, to switch to a Judeo-Christian image, if it is true that we are all dependent on each other, we cannot allow starvation or malnourishment of the poor or any part of the body without hurting the whole body. We will have to proclaim release to the captives because every part is needed for the proper functioning of the whole. There must be recovery of sight to the blind because all the parts must have all their senses about them. And those who are oppressed must be set at liberty, because a body can in no sense be healthy if it is fighting with itself, spending all its energies on internal warfare.

This philosophical perspective would result in factories producing trucks and tractors as opposed to warheads, in a concern for inner integrity, cooperation, and wholeness as opposed to outer recognition, hoarding, and the fearful dramas of fragmentation.

> *If a nation is centered in the Tao,*
> *if it nourishes its own people*
> *and doesn't meddle in the affairs of others,*
> *it will be a light to all nations in the world.*
> *(Mitchell, 61)*

Here is an example that illustrates the cost of not finding ways to embody these principles, which are easier to speak of than to practice. Nate was working as a psychological counselor at a downtown job-training center that served mainly minority clients in a large metropolitan area. Nate's job was to work with clients who had low self-esteem or other psychological issues that interfered with their performance in the training program. After three years it became clear that the work of the center in general, and Nate in particular, was not especially productive. Officials questioned whether it was wise or efficient to continue the work. As often happens, a study was commissioned to find out why a good enough idea in itself (providing job training) was not working.

The most general conclusion of the study was that the center was predestined for failure because it addressed only a small part of the issue, with insufficient attention to the whole in which it was inextricably bound up. Nate's job, for instance, was predicated on the assumption that self-esteem and motivation are a purely individual matter that can be dealt with through working with a skilled counselor. The study demonstrated that this was a hopelessly simplistic assumption.

For one thing, Nate's clients did not believe they had a chance of finding a good job after training. Minorities in the metropolitan area were not being hired for anything but minimum-salary jobs. There was documentable discrimination that showed minority men and women were rarely promoted to higher-paying jobs. Unions were letting in very few minority applicants, even though they were qualified. Nate's clients were not convinced that working to get high school equivalency certificates was a sure route out of their ghetto situation. Getting all the way through college seemed a far-off dream indeed.

Even those who were motivated to work on their inner attitudes with Nate found it hard to make appointments with him. It was a time of fast growth and redevelopment within the metropolitan area. A great number of apartments and homes had been torn down to make way for large business developments. A vast, sprawling public housing development had been built in a former farming area outside the city limits. A number of Nate's clients who were relocated there in the new row apartments discovered a transportation problem. There were no stores and shops within walking distance and the transit system connecting them to the city center was poor and costly. If a client could get to Nate after managing the transportation problem, there was often a child-care problem. People who relocated in the housing development were often separated from their extended families and old friends who had previously helped out with child care. Children left alone in the housing development often got into trouble. Although thousands of housing units were put in, with multiple families living in one apartment, no park or recreation area was provided. Developers and metropolitan officials said land was too valuable to allocate to recreational uses. So, children began playing in the streets, stripping cars, and getting involved with drugs and prostitution at younger and younger ages. They were bused to schools at significant distances from the development, so there were few after-school activities they could join in with new friends from school.

Nate and his colleagues soon recognized their clients' transit problem and applied for additional funding to address it. Officials were hesitant to put more funds into an already costly program before it had proved its worth. The center staff knew that many small businesses which would benefit from the personnel they were training were not big enough to support their own child-care facilities for those parents in the program. The center tried to mobilize an innovative plan in which a dozen small businesses could share the cost of a jointly run child-care facility. There was interest in the idea, but little concrete progress after a year of discussions.

Gene, a friend of Nate, who had both friends and family in the new housing development, decided to do something about all the kids who were getting into trouble there. The development was providing five times the number of youths in the state juvenile justice system than would be predicted from its percentage of children in the state population. Gene moved into the development and began work with a $6,000 grant from a church agency. He put together a basketball court on a back lot and organized a nine-team league with over one hundred kids. He sponsored an all-comers track meet for those two to ninety-two years old through closing off a portion of a street for a makeshift stadium. He asked a nearby service organization to provide prizes for everyone who participated. He began classes for children in what to do when coming home to empty houses after school. He convinced one person to start a computer club, another to put on a musical, a nearby church to start a scout troop, a judge to use him for providing alternative sentences, and more. After six months the number of youths in the juvenile justice system had gone down 30 percent. The director of the county juvenile justice program recognized the value of what Gene was doing, since the cost to the public for keeping one youth in a correctional facility was over $36,000 a year, not including costs for local police, probation officers, private and public attorneys, and the courts. The director diverted another $14,000 of federal funds into Gene's program to keep it going. After nine months the number of youths in the justice system had dropped by 45 percent. After a year the church grant, which was allocated only for start-up money for new programs, ran out. The federal money for primary prevention programs was cut off as politicians on all levels ran on "get tough with crime" platforms that ended up putting more police on the streets, at a cost of over $50,000 a year per officer, and building more costly jail cells.

In summary, the cost to the community of not coordinating its efforts in addressing its overall problems was enormous. Not providing transportation, child care, and a better climate for economically just race relations resulted in the loss of a great deal of money put into an ineffective job training center. Nate's psychological counseling was limited to a supportive as opposed to transformative function. Businesses were not provided with a valuable source of personnel. New potential consumers, who could get off the public assistance rolls, were not developed and nurtured. Not providing recreational areas and money for preventive programs in the housing development put a tremendous financial burden on the area to pay for legal, correctional, medical, and related services. People walked the streets in fear as the crime rate went up. Racial and class antagonisms increased. Politicians focused attention abroad on such things as unfair trade practices, repressive regimes, and human rights violations, insisting that their community, for all its minor problems, was still the best place on earth. The cost of allowing the poor, disabled, and oppressed to continue in their plight brought a sickness to the communal, metropolitan body and beyond, which was not clearly seen or understood, but which touched the lives of every person in the community.

Individually and socially, the Tao teaches us harshly through allowing us to experience the consequences of our own actions.

When the world is governed according to Tao,
Horses are used to work on the farm.
When the world is not governed according to Tao,
Horses and weapons are produced for the frontier.
No crime is greater than that of ambition.
No misfortune is greater than that of discontentment.
No fault is greater than that of conquering.
(Chang, 46)

FOSTERING VIRTUE

玄德

All things arise from Tao.
They are nourished by Virtue.
They are formed from matter.
They are shaped by environment.
Thus the ten thousand things all respect Tao
and honor Virtue.
Respect of Tao and honor of Virtue are
not demanded,
But they are in the nature of things.
(Feng & English, 51)

Psychotherapy is sometimes portrayed as a process in which ethical questions are suspended, feelings are fostered as opposed to virtue, and anything outside of physical harm to another is allowed. However, psychotherapy is always a value-laden enterprise. Everything a psychotherapist does reveals a conscious or unconscious set of values and beliefs. The teaching of Lao Tzu is that each of us is endowed with virtue. Ideally, every mature person should be able to recognize what is appropriate and instinctively be moved to do it. Psychotherapy in the tradition of Lao Tzu involves itself with issues of maturity and virtue through exploring the question of how our perceptions and actions are organized. Do we correctly see our interdependence with all life, and live a life of gratitude and compassion? Or does our consciousness organize our experience and expression through all sorts of fearful, distorting illusions that lead us into harmful ways? Do we know on more than an intellectual level that,

> *Every being in the universe [including ourselves] is an expression of the Tao?*
> *(Mitchell, 51)*

Or do we think our claim to fame is in being beautiful, smart, rich, or right, in which case we will need to make sure there are those we can point to who are ugly, stupid, poor, and wrong?

Taoist psychotherapists have little faith that the conscious level of people's understanding of morality will guide them in ethical binds.

> *The more taboos and inhibitions there are in the world,*
> *The poorer the people become.*
> *The sharper the weapons the people possess,*

The greater confusion reigns in the realm. . . .
The more articulate the laws and ordinances,
The more robbers and thieves arise.
(Wu, 57)

When the country is governed through harshness and sharp
investigation,
The people are more deceitful and dishonest.
(Chang, 58)

When they lose their sense of awe,
people turn to religion.
When they no longer trust themselves,
they begin to depend on authority.
(Mitchell, 72)

The psychotherapeutic process suggested here hopes to reinstate awe through encouraging trust in the inner authority of our own experience which can reconnect us with ourselves and the world around us. It is only the self-authenticating experience of our inner "yes!" that gives substance to words of virtue, although the words by themselves may be valid.

Does this mean that to transform ourselves into paragons of virtue all we have to do is encourage a little inner awareness? No. It takes a great deal of, as opposed to just a little, awareness. There are stages to negotiate, and also the

quality of our communal life and relationships makes a crucial difference. For example, at first a little inner awareness
led June, a woman with few friends, to recognize a slight
uneasiness around new people. Staying with the inner exploration led to an involuntary terror and rage at letting
others get too close. Memories of being used and abused
arose. The decision of the young child to be strong and
maintain a position of power in relation to others became
conscious. June's inner wisdom led her to the source of her
pain. It would have been unusual, however, for June to come
this far without the presence of a therapist who trusted in
creation in general and the wisdom of June's fears and hesita-
tions in particular.

In the next stage, the therapist invited June to observe
what it was like to consider the possibility of allowing closeness with people who would not use it against her. Barriers
automatically arose, activated by her early pain and fear.
Each barrier was attended to, to discover what was necessary
to allow in the new possibility. No negativity, no fear or
defense against the notion of closeness, was overridden.
Transformation eventually happened when June was able to
acknowledge that it is both good and possible to allow closeness with *some* people, *some* of the time. Acknowledging this
new possibility was an actual experience for her with the
therapist and with some others in the group. She retained the

knowledge that some (though not all) people do use closeness and vulnerability to manipulate for greater power, and she knew she could always use her ability to defend against them.

In terms of fostering virtue, it was important that she became more conscious and compassionate about her own life's pilgrimage and the way she had organized herself around power issues. She had a taste of the wonder of more intimate relational possibilities, the meaning and joy they can bring. Her compassion was then able to begin extending to others who could be manipulative or exploitive.

The importance cannot be underestimated of the therapist, her group, and the community June returned to for supporting her new growth. Asian thought in general, as well as Lao Tzu in particular, has never elevated the autonomous ego above the community. Community is foundational for the individual. That is why Lao Tzu offered advice for those who influence community through governance. Again, we are led back to the very being of the therapist and others we have close contact with. Modeling and relationships are more influential than is correct analysis. An infant learns a language by growing up surrounded by a community that speaks the language, not by being instructed in grammatical rules. In the same way, if we want more sanity, wholeness, and virtue, this is best accomplished by living in community with those who embody these principles.

Therefore all things arise from Tao.
By Virtue they are nourished,
Developed, cared for,
Sheltered, comforted,
Grown, and protected.
Creating without claiming,
Doing without taking credit,
Guiding without interfering,
This is Primal Virtue.
(Feng & English, 51)

UNMASKING

The great Way is a very level road,
But men like to take circuitous paths.
Thus, the palaces are extremely elegant,
But the people's farms are extremely desolate,
And there is no grain reserved in the
storehouses.
The rulers wear expensive garments,
Carry fine swords,
Satiate themselves with food and drink,
And possess inordinate riches and
precious things.
This is the greatest robbery,
And is indeed against the great Way.
(Chang, 53)

Lao Tzu teaches that it takes awareness to escape from the trances that our cultures induce so that we can relinquish the masks which prevent us from living the truth. Part of our predicament in so doing is that we do not encounter the world in a state that the European philosopher Martin Heidegger called "releasement consciousness." We do not have eyes to see, ears to hear. Our masks not only prevent others from seeing us, they distort our own perception. We do not recognize and appreciate perfection, fullness, beauty, or pain when they are present. We are not mindful. Part of this is because our consciousness has been overlaid with the filters of a particular culture, the coloring mythos of an entire era. Perhaps we have been entranced by the lure of extreme elegance, expensive garments, and fine swords.

Therapy encourages our communion with a greater spectrum of realities. It releases our consciousness to greater freedom of perception. Our awareness is turned inward or outward toward present, concrete experience. To accomplish this exploration, we have to suspend our automatic judgments, opinions, and cultural learning. As we integrate what we discover, we have the opportunity to compare our experience with that of our heritage. We can decide if our tradition's expression and framing of life's realities fit our personal findings. We can never jump out of our cultural setting to some supposedly neutral, objective standpoint, but we can open ourselves to a dialogue with our tradition in which we choose what seems appropriate while at the same time stretching its boundaries and contours where need be.

Whatever our heritage, in releasement consciousness, which may also be called mindfulness, we have the opportunity to discover along with the writer-philosopher W. H. Hudson that being released to see a single blade of grass contains more wonder and promise than immersion in a deluge of the latest fads and fashions. We can even learn to savor and luxuriate in the experience of wearing a new coat or driving a finely engineered car so that we have no need to fantasize about some other car or coat. We can appreciate the moment for what it is and also what it is not. We can be nourished by its fullness and perfection, which can also give us the freedom to see the distortions of the cultural maskings around us.

> *If I had even a slight awareness,*
> *And practiced the great Way,*
> *What I would fear would be deviating from it.*
> (Chang, 53)

EXPANDING

What is well planted cannot be uprooted. . . .

Cultivate Virtue in your own person,
And it becomes a genuine part of you.
Cultivate it in the family,
And it will abide.
Cultivate it in the community,
And it will live and grow.
Cultivate it in the state,
And it will flourish abundantly.
Cultivate it in the world,
And it will become universal.
(Wu, 54)

One of the strong cultural myths that needs to be unmasked in the West is that of the acultural, ahistorical, apolitical individual. In the West we have uncritically promoted the notion of the individual who can create personal meaning independent of social entanglements, separate from binding family emotional ties, transcend the crises of life objectively and dispassionately without any dependencies, face suffering without avoidance and death without denial, and more—all through actualizing the powers of the fully realized, autonomous self. Viewed cross-culturally, this Western celebration of the self is seen as both illusory and tyrannical, totally ignoring the reality of individuals developing inseparably from their social and cultural contexts, as was illustrated in the chapter "Broadening Horizons," earlier. As Lao Tzu suggests in chapter 54, virtue, the ability to live in right relationship with ourselves and the world around us, must be cultivated and take deep root in the individual, but to be truly well planted it must extend to family, community, state, and world.

The style of therapy we have explored in this book of moving from dialogue about our stories in ordinary consciousness to studying our inner experience in a mindful state of consciousness, was never meant to be limited to the context of individual therapy, though this could be easily assumed in our Western world. One exception to individual work is those of us who have lived through some kind of trauma, such as a war or childhood sexual abuse. Though personal therapy may be appropriate in part, we also need to find a group of like survivors with whom we can share our stories. It is important to have our experience confirmed by others who have gone through the same thing, notice the similarities between their experience and ours, realize that we made the best accommodation possible at the time, and receive group support for doing whatever is necessary to heal our personal lives and to influence public measures necessary for the healing of the greater society. To do only individual therapy in relation to such traumas implies that the problem is in us and leaves out the communal dimensions.

Another qualification applies to those of us who are living in a serious, long-term relationship. When we feel we want to explore some aspect of our life with a therapist, it is preferable that our partner come with us. Some therapists even make that a requirement. The technical term for this is conjoint relationship therapy. It is important because, *Lone Ranger* movies to the contrary, we do not live life as independent, uninfluenced egos. The forces that draw us together as a couple are powerful and partly unconscious. The quality of the emotional home base we set up with each other exerts a profound influence on our lives.

There are many advantages to exploring personal life issues in the presence of our loved ones. For instance, it can deepen their compassion and understanding of who we are. It can clarify for them how they activate our fears. It gives them greater insight into how to support the directions we need to grow in. It can help them realize that we came to the relationship with a great deal of baggage and personal history that has nothing to do with them. This can help them not take everything we say or do so personally, and not worry so much about what they may be doing to stimulate unpleasant reactions in us. Even if we are the ones who initially present ourselves as troubled or searching to a therapist, if we bring our partners along, it usually does not take long for them to start exploring themselves also, so that two-way appreciation and empathy occurs.

Sometimes, of course, our relationship is so hurtful and defensive that there is not enough respect and safety for us to explore ourselves in the presence of the other. Then a therapist may need to see us individually and schedule joint appointments when appropriate. In either case, the issues that relating to someone close to us stir up are often the richest in terms of stimulating learning and growth. That assumes, of course, that we are willing to look at our own part in a relationship and not simply assume that the other person is the one who is wrong and needs to change. If we do choose to see a therapist by ourselves, we should be aware of the danger, which is that we may begin changing in a way that is threatening and difficult to understand for our partner. When we change, the original contract or bond that brought us together changes. This leads to the possibility of a rift in our relationship, or to deepening the rift that has already begun. Sometimes, however, especially if we are in what is called a "co-dependent" posture with someone—that is, if we are inappropriately protecting and accommodating their needs and destructive behavior—going ahead on our own is the best thing we can do for ourselves, the other person, and the relationship.

The general wisdom of Lao Tzu is that all things come from the Tao and therefore everything is connected to everything else. If one thing changes, everything changes. The changes in an individual can affect a family or neighborhood. A political or economic change in a community can affect an individual. This kind of systems logic is the basis of family therapy. A therapist might suggest to us that it is beneficial to include various members of our family in one or more sessions. Sometimes, especially when therapy involves working with young people, it can be beneficial to include as many parts of a relational system as possible: teachers, school counselors, employers, pastors, coaches, juvenile court counselors, friends, and neighbors as well as family members.

At whatever level of complexity our web of relationships is being explored, the principles of respectful, mindful therapy flowing from Tao can be followed. A marriage, family, or community can step back and take itself under observation in a similar way that we can as individuals. To be productive, any level of work requires the willingness to empty ourselves of what we think we want and know, and a corresponding willingness to open ourselves to what emerges as important and needful.

> *The Way of Heaven is to benefit others and not to injure.*
> *The Way of the sage is to act but not to compete.*
> *(Chan, 81)*

CONCLUSION

He who grasps anything loses it. . . .

[The Sage] only helps all creatures to
find their own nature,
But does not venture to lead them by
the nose.
(Wu, 64)

He simply reminds people
of who they have always been.
(Mitchell, 64)

Lao Tzu gives us much to ponder and embody along the Way as we seek to foster
virtue in our families, neighborhoods, and
various communities:

Because he has given up helping,
he is people's greatest help.
(Mitchell, 78)

The Master's power is like this.
He lets all things come and go

effortlessly, without desire.
(Mitchell, 55)

Humility means trusting the Tao,
thus never needing to be defensive.
(Mitchell, 61)

Compassionate toward yourself,
you reconcile all beings in the world.
(Mitchell, 67)

Can any of us, therapists, clients or both, hope to attain to such wisdom, to such a quality of being-in-the-world? No. To attain anything implies an effortful, usually self-centered attempt that separates us from what we seek before we start. While we may not be able to attain, the *Tao-te ching* does suggest a possibility that we might allow some healing experiences to happen. Lao Tzu affirms a creation in which we can be content, one that provides more than enough for our needs, one that we do not have to change, a creation in which reconciliation occurs as we find compassion for ourselves and others. Perhaps with some encouragement from a therapist, friend, group, or guide we can open ourselves to the possibility that the creation can nourish us. Instead of fighting it, we may discover a way to be at peace with it and creatively enter into its rhythms.

Mindfulness is a wonderful tool for exploring creation and letting it into our lives. As we watch carefully, we not only become witness to and let go of unnecessary attachments, we identify with that part of our mind which is awareness itself. When we are in such a state of "not knowing" anything in particular, we may experience unity and interrelatedness. This place of unselfconscious compassion is a state that is beyond therapy.

Whatever happens along the Way, therapists will continue to be greatly blessed when we allow them to share our pilgrimage. Therapists are continually moved, enriched, and taught by those who come to them in their journey toward awareness, truth, and meaningful living.

Much more could be said. However, as this little volume has endeavored to suggest, it is not helpful to talk about something too much. It is better to enter directly into experience—walking in the park, tending the garden, relating to the boss, hugging a child, or trying therapy—and see if the guidance of Lao Tzu is confirmed by our own inner wisdom.

How do I know about the world?
By what is within me.
(Wu, 54)

Blessings.

The Tao nourishes by not forcing.
By not dominating, the Master leads.
(Mitchell, 81)

天之道利而不害
聖人之道為而不爭

KEY TO
CHINESE CHARACTERS

The characters were chosen by Charles Chu from the Chinese text of the Tao-te ching *referred to in each chapter.*

A NOTE ABOUT THE AUTHORS AND THE ARTIST

Greg Johanson is a certified therapist and senior trainer of the Hakomi Institute as well as editor of the *Hakomi Forum*. An ordained United Methodist minister, he has over twenty years clinical, teaching, and training experience in parish, mental health clinic, college, hospital, and workshop settings. He has published more than seventy-five items in the field of pastoral theology and psychotherapy. He lives with his wife, Hope, and son, Leif, in northwest New Jersey.

Ron Kurtz is the founder and director of the Hakomi Institute. He developed Hakomi in the mid-1970s as the culmination of years of study and experience with psychology, body-centered psychotherapies, the intellectual breakthroughs of modern systems theory, and the spiritual principles of Taoism and Buddhism. He has led workshops throughout North America and Europe and is the author of *Body-Centered Psychotherapy: The Hakomi Method* and co-author (with Hector Prestera, M.D.) of *The Body Reveals*. He lives with his wife, Terry, and daughter, Lily, in southwest Oregon.

Charles Chu is Professor Emeritus of Chinese and Curator of the Chu-Griffis Art Collection at Connecticut College. In 1945 he came to the United States and received an M.A. in political science from the University at Berkeley. He has taught at the Army Language School in Monterey and at Yale. In 1965 he established at Connecticut College the first approved undergraduate major in Chinese language and literature in a private liberal arts college. He lives with his wife, Bettie, in New London.

Information about therapy and training resources of the Hakomi Institute can be obtained through its home office: P.O. Box 1873, Boulder, CO 80306. Telephone: (303) 443-6209.

Other Bell Tower Books

Valeria Alfeyeva. PILGRIMAGE TO DZHVARI: *A Woman's Journey of Spiritual Awakening.* Hardcover 0-517-59194-4 (1993)

David A. Cooper. SILENCE, SIMPLICITY, AND SOLITUDE: *A Guide for Spiritual Retreat.* Hardcover 0-517-58620-7 (1992)

———. THE HEART OF STILLNESS: *The Elements of Spiritual Practice.* Hardcover 0-517-58621-5 (1992)

James G. Cowan. LETTERS FROM A WILD STATE: *Rediscovering Our True Relationship to Nature.* Hardcover 0-517-58770-X (1992)

———. MESSENGERS OF THE GODS: *Tribal Elders Reveal the Ancient Wisdom of the Earth.* Softcover 0-517-88078-4 (1993)

Marc David. NOURISHING WISDOM: *A Mind/Body Approach to Nutrition and Well-Being.* Hardcover 0-517-57636-8 (1991); Softcover 0-517-88129 (1994)

Noela N. Evans. MEDITATIONS FOR THE PASSAGES AND CELEBRATIONS OF LIFE: *A Book of Vigils.* Hardcover 0-517-59341-6 (1994)

Jack and Marcia Kelly. SANCTUARIES—THE NORTHEAST: *A Guide to Lodgings in Monasteries, Abbeys, and Retreats of the United States.* Softcover 0-517-57727-5 (1991)

———. SANCTUARIES—THE WEST COAST AND SOUTHWEST. Softcover 0-517-88007-5 (1993)

———. ONE HUNDRED GRACES, eds. Hardcover 0-517-58567-7 (1992)

Barbara Lachman. THE JOURNAL OF HILDEGARD OF BINGEN. Hardcover 0-517-59169-3 (1993)

Gunilla Norris. BEING HOME: *A Book of Meditations.* Hardcover 0-517-58159-0 (1991)

———. BECOMING BREAD: *Meditations on Loving and Transformation.*
Hardcover 0-517-59168-5 (1993)

———. SHARING SILENCE: *Meditation Practice and Mindful Living.*
Hardcover 0-517-59506-0 (1993)

Ram Dass and Mirabai Bush. COMPASSION IN ACTION: *Setting Out on the Path of Service.* Softcover 0-517-57635-X (1992)

Richard Whelan, ed. SELF-RELIANCE: *The Wisdom of Ralph Waldo Emerson as Inspiration for Daily Living.* Softcover 0-517-58512-X (1991)

Bell Tower books are for sale at your local bookstore, or you may order with a credit card by calling 1-800-733-3000.